THE SADDLEBRED
America's Horse of Distinction

THE SADDLEBRED

America's Horse of Distinction

Photographed by TODD BUCHANAN

Historical Research by LYNN P. WEATHERMAN

Published by
JUDY FISHER OETINGER

Dedicated to
my parents, John and Janice Fisher
and to Marcella Lahr — who in many ways
made this book possible.

Additional Photography by:

American Saddlebred Horse Association - Page 143
Historical photographs courtesy of the American Saddle Horse
Museum and the American Saddlebred Association.
Doug Bartholomew - Pages 91, 95 (top right), 101 (bottom)
Alix Coleman - Page 124 (top) Avis Girdler - Page 76 (top right)
Sandra Hall - American Saddlebred Horse Association - Page 130 (top)
Sari Levin - Page 76 (top left), 96 (top) John Schiedt - Pages 4-5
William Strode - Pages 96 (bottom right), l05 (bottom)
Charles Westerman - Donna Lawrence Productions - Page 148

Executive Editors: William Butler and William Strode
Library of Congress Catalog Number: 90-84750
Hardcover International Standard Book Number 0-9l6509-79-6
Color Separations by Gateway Press, Louisville, Kentucky,
Printed by Arcata Graphics, Kingsport, Tennesse
First Edition printed Fall, 1991 by Harmony House Publishers,
P.O. Box 90, Prospect, Kentucky 40059 (502) 228-2010 / 228-4446
Copyright © 1991 by Judy Fisher Oetinger
Photographs copyright © 1991 by Todd Buchanan, except where noted.

Cover design taken from the original watercolor "Saddlebred:
Performing Arts" by James L. Crow, courtesy
of the American Saddle Horse Museum's Collection.

Confederate cavalrymen, who usually supplied their own horses for combat, often rode Saddlebreds. This monument, which depicts a horse soldier on a Saddlebred, is at the Gettysburg, Pennsylvania Civil War battlefield.

CONTENTS

Yearlings at Callaway Hills Stable, Jefferson City, Missouri. Callaway Hills is one of the largest Saddlebred breeding farms in the United States.

FOREWORD

By Pat Nichols
Executive Secretary, ASHA

he 1991 publication date of *The Saddlebred: America's Horse of Distinction* is particularly fitting because it is the Centennial year of the American Saddlebred Horse Association.

While early Saddlebred-type horses had undergone various stages of development during the preceding century, it was not until 1891 that a registry for the breed was established in Louisville, Kentucky. The National Saddle Horse Breeders Association, the first non-privately owned registry for an American native breed, was founded that year under the leadership of the distinguished U.S. Army General John B. Castleman.

For a time, great rivalry existed between Missouri and Kentucky for recognition as Saddle Horse breeding centers. General Castleman, realizing that union between the two groups was essential, made several trips to Mexico, Missouri, to convince Missourians of the need to support the burgeoning national association and to lay aside regional differences and plans to form a separate Missouri association.

That Castleman was successful is evident. The American Saddlebred Horse Association (the erstwhile NSHBA) relocated from Louisville to the richly historic Bluegrass region of Lexington, Kentucky. The Association now registers Saddlebreds born all over the world, administers prize programs, produces videos, and engages in a variety of activities for both youth and adults. Publications include newsletters and a bimonthly magazine.

The Saddle Horse Museum exhibits relate the history of the breed in a lively and interesting way, and featured is an award-winning multimedia slide show. The museum has a collection of works by George Ford Morris, the respected equine artist, and a stunning Patricia Crane bronze statue in front of the museum marks the grave of the memorable breeding stallion Supreme Sultan (d. 1983). An extensive research library is also housed at the museum building.

In Mexico, Missouri, at the 1870 mansion known as Graceland, the Audrain County Historical Society also maintains an American Saddle Horse Museum, especially noteworthy for its multitude of regional artifacts, primitive paintings, and the portrayal of the engaging life story of the great black trainer Tom Bass. Bass (d. 1934) was a Saddlebred legend who surmounted racial barriers with his superb horsemanship. The remains of Mexico's most celebrated horse, the five-gaited champion stallion Rex McDonald (d. 1913), are buried on the grounds.

Both Missouri and Kentucky continue to be important Saddlebred territory. But, as the images of *The Saddlebred: America's Horse of Distinction* clearly show, Saddlebreds are now seen all over the country — on mountain trails, city streets, bridle paths, in back yards and in show arenas. Wouldn't General Castleman be pleased to know how far his beloved breed has traveled since 1891?

Chief of Longview

INTRODUCTION

by Judy Fisher Oetinger

Many years of trying to explain the American Saddlebred and to rectify misconceptions about the breed to other horse admirers have given me the idea of putting together a book that could tell the history of the breed in a short, concise manner. I have attempted to give the reader information on details like conformation, bits and shoeing and through photography show the American Saddlebred as it really is — a beautiful, athletic, intelligent, working horse, that performs with as much style, dignity and versatility as any breed in the world.

With that in mind, last year I approached two fine gentlemen who enthusiastically embraced my idea and helped make it a reality — Bill Butler and Bill Strode of Harmony House Publishers in Louisville, Kentucky.

With their guidance, Todd Buchanan was selected to photograph the book. Talent alone would have been enough to make him an excellent choice. His work has been featured in newspapers and magazines for years. But the fact that he is a former equitation champion and that he agreed that a book on Saddlebreds was long overdue, made him an ideal person for the job. Next, I went to the American Saddlebred Horse Association and announced my intentions to do this book . . . could they help? Not only did the entire staff give their support, but through their incredible efforts we pulled together all the information needed for the book.

I will be forever grateful to Pat Nichols, executive secretary to the ASHA, for her great support and ever-watchful eye, making sure all our information was correct and up to the high standards of the ASHA.

Lynn Weatherman, editor of *The American Saddlebred* and a fine writer and Saddlebred historian, contributed so much time and knowledge to this project that I can never thank him enough.

I would be remiss if I did not thank Marcella Lahr for her love and devotion to the breed and for building the same love in her many students who went on to win championships and awards because of her efforts. She is as sharp and informative as anyone in the business, and her training has helped me build the foundation for meeting perfection requirements in many facets of life.

A note: the photographs you see in this work are but a fraction of the many horses, owners, trainers and riders that we photographed for the book. I am sorry that we could not use every one of them, but space limitations made that impossible. But from the pictures that were chosen I hope you will be able to experience a little of the excitement of the show ring and the activity within it; understand the many facets of Saddlebred care and preparation; and sense some of the pure pleasure of riding a Saddlebred horse.

Maybe the book will instill a bit of adventure in those who haven't yet experienced the Saddlebred horse world and will intrigue them enough to venture forth with the rest of us to share the thrill.

Edna May

THE AMERICAN SADDLEBRED HORSE

ver 250 years of selective breeding have given us the beautiful, all-purpose riding horse called the American Saddlebred. While many people around the world recognize this horse for its aesthetic and athletic feats in the show ring, the Saddlebred is now perceived as a breed that can excel in many other equine specialities — such as multi-purpose family horses, working and trail horses, dressage horses, jumpers, and harness and carriage horses.

Saddlebreds can trace their roots back to Europe, specifically to the natural-gaited Galloway and Hobbie horses that survived the treacherous Atlantic passage in the immigration from Great Britain to America in the mid-1600s. Hardiness in those breeds enabled them not only to survive, but to thrive in America. After a period of selective breeding, a new type of horse was developed from them in the Rhode Island area near Naragansett Bay. Called "Naragansett Pacers," they were soon found up and down the eastern seaboard, with a concentration in Virginia.

For all practical purposes, the Naragansett Pacer is now extinct, due to a mass exportation of the breed to the West Indies. The Paso Fino is probably a direct descendant of the Naragansett, though, and resembles it closely. But before they were all gone, Naragansett mares were crossed with Thoroughbreds which arrived in America from England in the early 1700s. By the time of the American Revolution, a horse simply called the "American" horse, had become a recognized type. These horses retained the size and beauty of Thoroughbreds, but had the inclination, or at least the ability, to learn the easy riding gaits. These animals quickly became popular in Colonial America for their versatility. They were used for general riding, for work, and for pulling carriages, and were prized for a pleasant temperament, eagerness, strength, and stamina.

These were the horses that carried colonial cavalry to battle with the British and pulled munitions wagons and mobile artillery. After the war, they were dispersed throughout the colonies and later carried the pioneers from Virginia through the Cumberland Gap to the rolling hills of central Kentucky.

The "American horse" was the immediate precursor of the American Saddlebred horse. There were continual crossings with Thoroughbreds at the turn of the century. By the early 1800s the first horse shows were held in Kentucky, Virginia, and Missouri, American Saddlebreds were frequently judged the winners due to their beauty, style, and utility.

Court Days

Bourbon King Sold

The development of Saddlebreds and horse shows are inextricably linked. There is a widely held misconception that the so-called "court day" activities in the county seats of Kentucky and Missouri were somehow predecessors of horse shows. In fact, the first horse shows were just that, often held at county fairs with other livestock competitions.

There was horse trading on court days, however. People came to town for circuit court proceedings, and it was only natural that buying, selling, and trading of everything from tools to horses would take place. Bourbon King, for example, was sold as a weanling at a Mt. Sterling, Kentucky court day; Stonewall King was sold as a weanling in Fulton, Missouri. These court days were like horse shows in that horses were shown to their best advantage up and down the street. The judges in these "shows" were the toughest judges of all — potential customers.

The Saddlebred as we know it today virtually appeared in the flesh of an 1851 foal named Gaines' Denmark, who was the get of Thoroughbred and pacing stock. The pacing cross produced a horse with an ambling, lateral gait, comfortable for the rider. This horse emerged with a new mentality as well — a near-human pride in its appearance and performance. These characteristics became evident to rural owners who began to meet at county fairs to show off their fancy animals. These gatherings gradually took on a life of their own and established a social foothold, if not a competitive one. Eventually the rules of horse shows were formalized, and the first "national" horse show was held in 1856 in conjunction with the St. Louis Fair. American Saddlebreds held a prominent place in that first show.

By the time of the Civil War, Saddlebreds were the most popular riding animals in America. They were used in great numbers for Confederate cavalrymen and demonstrated incredible endurance and dependability on long marches and under fire. Generals on both sides proudly rode Saddlebreds.

Soldiers returning from the Civil War dispersed Saddlebreds far and wide. This was a versatile horse after all, and soon the breed could be found everywhere — on small midwestern farms, on the bridle paths in Central Park in New York City and on the plains of Texas herding cattle.

Saddlebred breeders then began serious negotiations to form a Saddle Horse association. The National Saddle Horse Breeders Association was organized on April 8, 1891, with the stated objective to "collect, record, and preserve pedigrees" and to attend to "other matters pertaining to the breeding, exhibition and sale" of Saddle Horses.

The march of time eventually diminished the utility of all horses, including the Saddlebred, and more and more its use was confined to horse shows, equine competitions, and general pleasure riding. Today the American Saddlebred is the ultimate show horse — elegant, beautiful, graceful, athletic and proud.

Robert E. Lee on Traveler, by Gray Eagle

National Saddle Horse Breeders Association formed

Developmental History of the American Saddlebred Horse

1776 American Horse
By the time of the American Revolution, an all-purpose, generic American Horse had been developed by crossing Naragansett "Native mares" with Thoroughbred stallions. These horses were larger and prettier than Naragansetts, but retained the easy gaits. The American Horse was first documented in a letter to the Continental Congress from an American diplomat in France in 1776. The Saddlebred type had been established.

Easy gaited horses were now virtually extinct in England. The singlefoot was lost after breeding to Oriental horses for several generations. The first Thoroughbred arrived from England on North American shores in 1706, about 18 years before the *Godolphin Barb* was foaled.

500-1500 AD Ancient English Pacer
These horses were the primary using animals throughout the British Isles in the Middle Ages (500-1500 A.D.). Generically known as palfreys, they were referred to in literature such as "The Canterbury Tales." Specific types were known by the location of their supposed source. Most notable were the Hobbies from Ireland and the Scotch Galloways. The Vikings, who used the northwest coasts of England and Ireland as staging areas for their long voyages, took them to Iceland from 874 to 930 A.D., and there they remain as the Icelandic, a breed noted for a very fast and pure rack. The term pace does not necessarily refer to a flat pace like today's Standardbred race horses but also to lateral movement such as an amble or singlefoot. The basic blood for the foundation of the American Saddlebred was from this ancient English horse. Gait was perhaps the overriding criterion for development of the breed until shortly before the founding of ASHA in 1891, and early registrations were based on the ability of a horse to perform the "saddle gaits."

1780
The westward migration of Americans stepped up following the Revolutionary War. These pioneers were carried by the best horses they could acquire, most of them either American Horses or Naragansetts.

1600s

1700s

1625 Galloways and Hobbies
Galloways and Hobbies were brought to North America by English colonists. Through selective breeding and improved nutrition, superior animals were developed by commercial breeders in Rhode Island and Virginia. These horses, called Naragansett Pacers after Rhode Island's famous Naragansett Bay, became the most popular horses in the Colonies.

1650 Naragansett Pacers
Naragansetts became a major commercial product and hundreds were sold to Spanish plantation owners in the West Indies. Because of a favorable tax situation, Canadians imported many Naragansetts. Colonists began breeding Naragansett mares to Thoroughbred stallions. The Naragansett population then began to diminish in the Colonies. It is thought that Paul Revere rode a Naragansett Pacer on his famous ride.

Naragansett Pacers had literally disappeared from the U.S. by 1820. They had been sold to sugar plantations on the Carribean islands. These same animals were the ancestors of today's Paso Finos. They also contributed to the gene pool of the Morgan and the Standardbred pacer. Those that went to Canada remained a repository of precious pacing blood, drawn upon by early Saddlebred breeders.

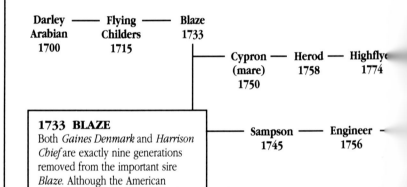

1733 BLAZE
Both *Gaines Denmark* and *Harrison Chief* are exactly nine generations removed from the important sire *Blaze*. Although the American Saddlebred had been established as a breed before the Denmarks and Chiefs entered the mainstream of the breed, some geneticists theorize that the cross-breeding of Denmarks and Chiefs set the breed in concrete.

1816 American Saddlebred
Horse shows were a popular form of entertainment and the first show on record was held near Lexington, Kentucky in 181▢ Kentucky horsemen quickly became commercial breeders. Continuing to add Thoroughbred blood to their easy-gaited horses they developed a larger, prettier all-purpose animal, setting fast the American Saddlebred as a breed. Each year, thousands of these horses were shipped south and east.

1650 Thoroughbreds
In England, roads began to improve, lessening the need for riding horses. Horse racing was a passion with British royalty, who began importing Arab, Barb, and Turkish stallions to cross on the native Hobbie and Galloway mares. This was the beginning of the Thoroughbred horse. The *Byerly Turk*, first of three stallions considered the Thoroughbred foundation sires, was foaled in 1679.

1800-1840
CANADIAN PACER
Canadian Pacers were probably simply Naragansett Pacers, some perhaps having crosses to French stock. *Tom Hal*, foaled in 1802 was imported from Canada and lived in Kentucky until 1843. *Copperbottom* was imported about 1812 and *Davy Crockett* in th 1830s. These three stallions were among the original 17 foundation sires designated when ASHA was formed.

1866
The Saddlebred industry recovered quickly from the Civil War because of the great demand for saddle horses and because Confederate veterans were allowed to keep the mounts they owned. Horse show competition became public entertainment and a major marketing tool.

1888
The rules for showing Saddlebreds were amended to require that horses show at the trot in addition to the "saddle gaits," the rack, running walk, fox trot and/or slow pace. The infusion of Chief blood became popular, giving the Saddlebred its great trot.

1890 Rex McDonald
Rex McDonald was foaled near Mexico, Missouri. He became one of the most famous and popular horses in America until the great Standard-bred pacer Dan Patch appeared on the national scene. *Rex McDonald* set the tone for American Saddlebreds.

1789 JUSTIN MORGAN
The American Morgan horse descended from one highly prepotent stallion of unknown parentage, *Justin Morgan*. While he and his sons stamped their get, it must be remembered that these horses had dams, some Naragansett and some Thorough-bred, whose qualities contributed to the Morgan breed before the time Morgan blood was infused into the Saddlebred.

Stockbridge Chief 1843 — Rattler 1854 — Peavine 1863

Sherman Morgan 1809 — Vermont Black Hawk 1833

Bloods Black Hawk 1847 — Indian Chief 1857

Gist's Black Hawk — Cabell's Lexington 1863

1800s   # 1900s

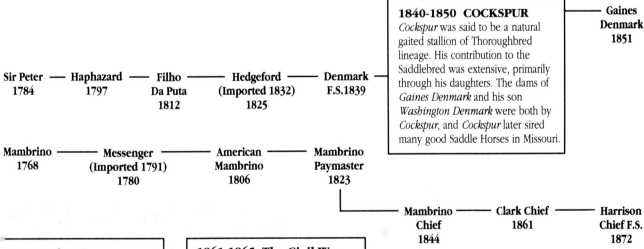

1840-1850 COCKSPUR
Cockspur was said to be a natural gaited stallion of Thoroughbred lineage. His contribution to the Saddlebred was extensive, primarily through his daughters. The dams of *Gaines Denmark* and his son *Washington Denmark* were both by *Cockspur*, and *Cockspur* later sired many good Saddle Horses in Missouri.

Gaines Denmark 1851

Sir Peter 1784 — Haphazard 1797 — Filho Da Puta 1812 — Hedgeford (Imported 1832) 1825 — Denmark F.S.1839

Mambrino 1768 — Messenger (Imported 1791) 1780 — American Mambrino 1806 — Mambrino Paymaster 1823

Mambrino Chief 1844 — Clark Chief 1861 — Harrison Chief F.S. 1872

1830-1860 The Highlanders
The Highlanders were Thor-oughbreds descended from the *Godolphin Barb*. They were important in the early develop-ment of the Saddlebred. *Black Squirrel*, through his dam, was an inbred Highlander. *Highland Chief*, the sire of *Mambrino LeGrand*, was by *Mambrino Chief* and out of a Highlander mare.

1856
The St. Louis Fair, which held the first horse show of national stature, was established.

1861-1865 The Civil War
The Civil War demonstrated the superiority of American Saddlebreds on the march and on the battlefield. Because of better horses, the Confederate cavalry dominated until remounts were impossible to obtain. Most high-ranking officers on both sides rode Saddlebred types.

1870 HACKNEY
Bellfounder was imported from England in 1822. This horse was a Hackney, often referred to in England as a Norfolk Trotter. The dam of Belle by *Latham's Denmark*, who produced *Bourbon Chief*, was said to be a granddaughter of *Bellfounder*.

1891
The American Saddlebred Horse Association was founded in Louisville, Kentucky, the first such organization for an American breed of horse. Originally known as the National Saddle-Horse Breeders Association, the name was changed to the American Saddle Horse Breeders Association in 1899 and to the American Saddlebred Horse Association in 1980, in order to better describe the horse and the all-encompassing mission of the Association.

1900 BOURBON KING
Bourbon King was foaled near Mt. Sterling, Kentucky. He became a sensational show horse and the great progenitor of the sire line of the Chief family of Saddlebreds.

Modern American Saddlebred
The American Saddlebred horse of today is primarily the result of crossing the Denmarks and the Chiefs.

Monte Cristo, Jr.

Monte Cristo, Jr., was the first registered American Saddlebred. Number one in the registry was bestowed on him for no particular honor, but most likely because of friendship between his owner J.T. Crenshaw of Shelby County, Kentucky, and Col I.B. Nall, the first ASHA secretary.

FOUNDATION SIRES

ourteen "Foundation Sires" were selected when the ASHA was established in 1891; three were added later. In 1902, seven were removed from the list, leaving ten, and in 1908, Denmark was recognized as the lone Foundation Sire. The other stallions were given regular registration numbers. Harrison Chief was recognized as the second Foundation Sire in 1991.

Denmark F.S. was foaled in 1839 at the Samuel Davenport farm, located two and a half miles from Danville, Kentucky.

There is little recorded history of Denmark and no paintings or photographs. James Farris, Lancaster, Kentucky, rode Betsey Harrison and exercised Denmark. He said Denmark stood sixteen hands, was dark brown in color and had a "long rangy neck with a 'gay tail'. His gaits were a fine walk, a slow pace, and he once ran in a 16 mile race at Lexington."

Col. John T. Hughes and James C. Graves said he had splendid conformation, was stylish with lofty carriage and had plenty of stamina and endurance. Most of his races were four miles.

A. B. Fant, Fulton, Missouri, formerly of Kentucky, said he had seen Denmark on many different occasions, that Denmark had sired many fine Saddle Horses, and that he purchased many of these good horses before the Civil War. Fant said he had sold 16 Denmark stallions to parties in Missouri and Illinois up until 1861.

Denmark stood at stud in Fayette County. Only three of his sons were registered: 1) Gaines' Denmark 61, whose contribution to the development of the American Saddlebred compared to that of Hambletonian in the development of the trotter; 2) Rob Roy 62, a very good show and breeding horse who died at age four or five, and 3) Muir's Denmark, who left many fine descendants.

While most American Saddlebreds trace to Denmark F.S. through Gaines Denmark, a few other unregistered sons and daughters produced registered get and are mentioned in the stud books. They include Miller's Denmark, Joe Blackburn, and the mare, Laura Dean.

Practically all registered American Saddlebred horses trace to Denmark F.S. The 1908 action of ASHA in designating him Foundation Sire was not misplaced. The first secretary, Col. I. B. Nall, once wrote, "Without Denmark, the Thoroughbred, where would we be in Saddle Horse breeding?"

Harrison Chief was a blood bay with no white markings. He grew to over sixteen hands, was full bodied with high head carriage and had a glorious full black tail which he seemed to carry higher each year. He was listed in John Wallace's Trotting Horse Register, established in 1871, and was considered a trotting horse throughout his life, although Saddle Horse men noted that every now and then his get could do the "saddle gaits."

Idolized by James Cromwell who called him

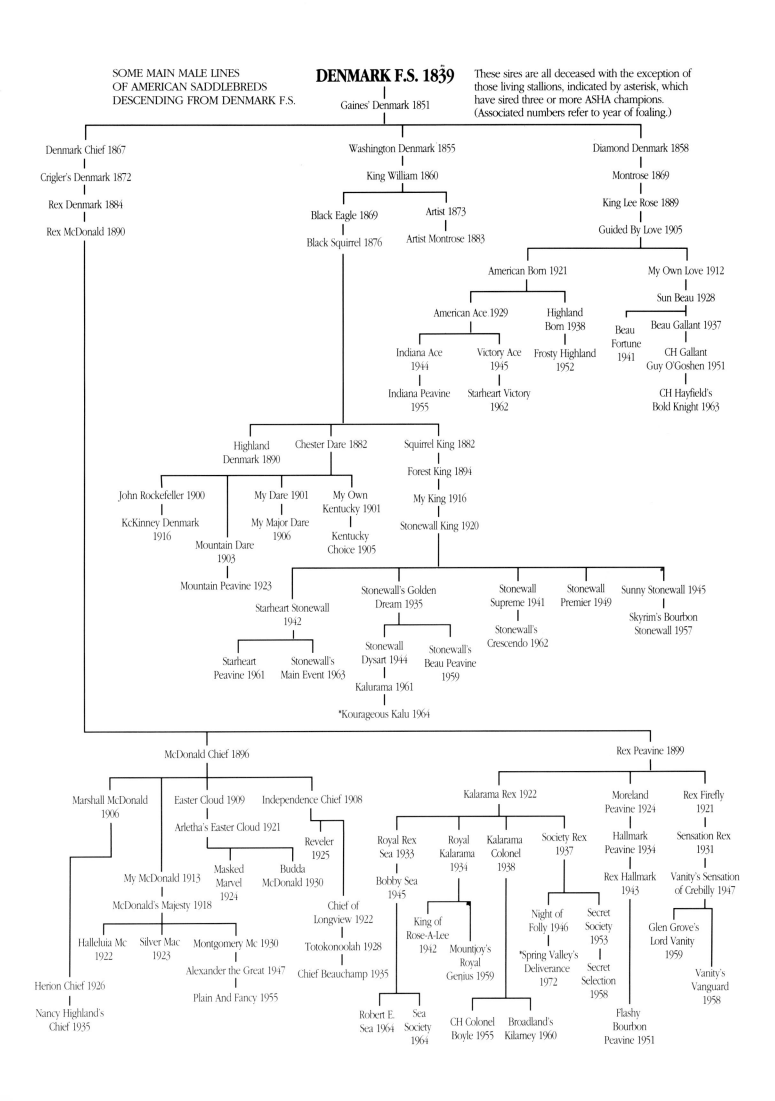

SOME MAIN MALE LINES
OF AMERICAN SADDLEBREDS
DESCENDING FROM DENMARK F.S.

DENMARK F.S. 1839

Gaines' Denmark 1851

These sires are all deceased with the exception of
those living stallions, indicated by asterisk, which
have sired three or more ASHA champions.
(Associated numbers refer to year of foaling.)

Denmark Chief 1867

Crigler's Denmark 1872

Rex Denmark 1884

Rex McDonald 1890

Washington Denmark 1855

King William 1860

Black Eagle 1869

Black Squirrel 1876

Artist 1873

Artist Montrose 1883

Diamond Denmark 1858

Montrose 1869

King Lee Rose 1889

Guided By Love 1905

American Born 1921

My Own Love 1912

Sun Beau 1928

American Ace 1929

Highland
Born 1938

Beau
Fortune
1941

Beau Gallant 1937

CH Gallant
Guy O'Goshen 1951

Indiana Ace
1944

Victory Ace
1945

Frosty Highland
1952

CH Hayfield's
Bold Knight 1963

Indiana Peavine
1955

Starheart Victory
1962

Highland
Denmark 1890

Chester Dare 1882

Squirrel King 1882

Forest King 1894

My King 1916

Stonewall King 1920

John Rockefeller 1900

KcKinney Denmark
1916

My Dare 1901

My Major Dare
1906

Mountain Dare
1903

My Own
Kentucky 1901

Kentucky
Choice 1905

Mountain Peavine 1923

Starheart Stonewall
1942

Stonewall's Golden
Dream 1935

Stonewall
Supreme 1941

Stonewall
Premier 1949

Sunny Stonewall 1945

Stonewall's
Crescendo 1962

Skyrim's Bourbon
Stonewall 1957

Starheart
Peavine 1961

Stonewall's
Main Event 1963

Stonewall
Dysart 1944

Stonewall's
Beau Peavine
1959

Kalurama 1961

*Kourageous Kalu 1964

McDonald Chief 1896

Rex Peavine 1899

Marshall McDonald
1906

Easter Cloud 1909

Arletha's Easter Cloud 1921

Independence Chief 1908

Kalarama Rex 1922

Moreland
Peavine 1924

Rex Firefly
1921

Reveler
1925

Masked
Marvel
1924

Budda
McDonald 1930

Royal Rex
Sea 1933

Royal
Kalarama
1934

Kalarama
Colonel
1938

Society Rex
1937

Hallmark
Peavine 1934

Sensation Rex
1931

My McDonald 1913

McDonald's Majesty 1918

Bobby Sea
1945

Rex Hallmark
1943

Vanity's Sensation
of Crebilly 1947

Chief of
Longview 1922

Halleluia Mc
1922

Silver Mac
1923

Montgomery Mc 1930

Alexander the Great 1947

Totokonoolah 1928

Chief Beauchamp 1935

King of
Rose-A-Lee
1942

Mountjoy's
Royal
Genius 1959

Night of
Folly 1946

Secret
Society
1953

Glen Grove's
Lord Vanity
1959

Herion Chief 1926

Plain And Fancy 1955

*Spring Valley's
Deliverance
1972

Secret
Selection
1958

Vanity's
Vanguard
1958

Nancy Highland's
Chief 1935

Robert E.
Sea 1964

Sea
Society
1964

CH Colonel
Boyle 1955

Broadland's
Kilarney 1960

Flashy
Bourbon
Peavine 1951

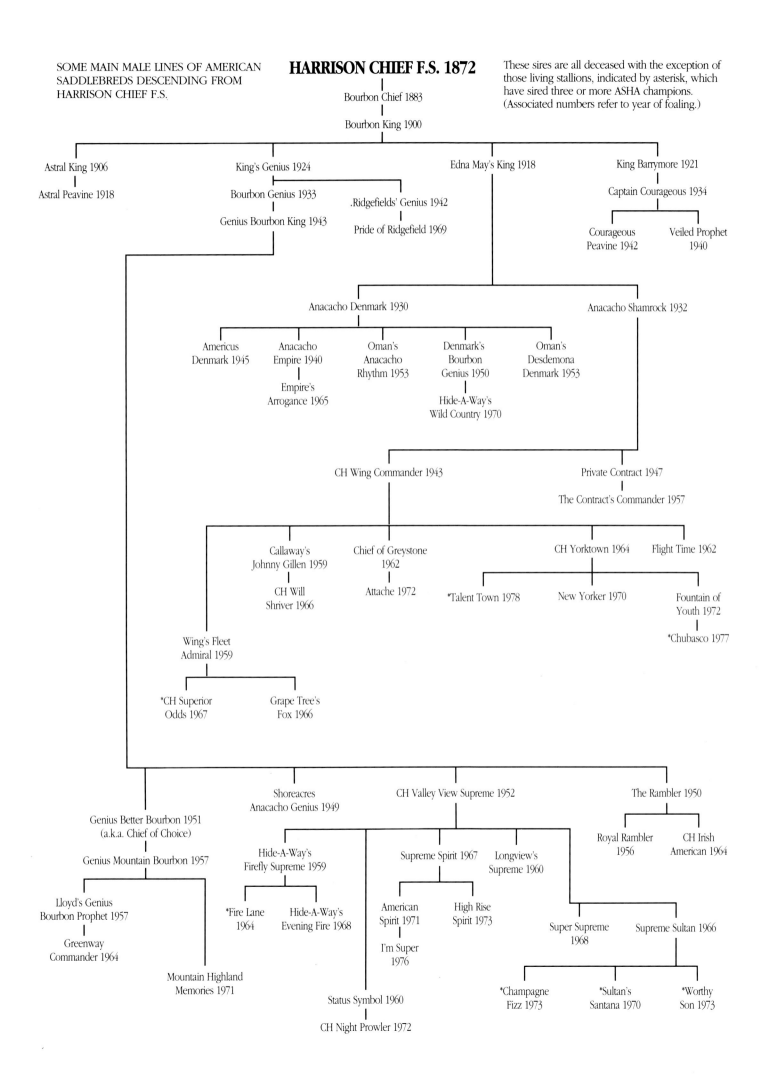

SOME MAIN MALE LINES OF AMERICAN SADDLEBREDS DESCENDING FROM HARRISON CHIEF F.S.

HARRISON CHIEF F.S. 1872

Bourbon Chief 1883

Bourbon King 1900

These sires are all deceased with the exception of those living stallions, indicated by asterisk, which have sired three or more ASHA champions. (Associated numbers refer to year of foaling.)

Astral King 1906

Astral Peavine 1918

King's Genius 1924

Bourbon Genius 1933

.Ridgefields' Genius 1942

Genius Bourbon King 1943

Pride of Ridgefield 1969

Edna May's King 1918

King Barrymore 1921

Captain Courageous 1934

Courageous Peavine 1942

Veiled Prophet 1940

Anacacho Denmark 1930

Anacacho Shamrock 1932

Americus Denmark 1945

Anacacho Empire 1940

Empire's Arrogance 1965

Oman's Anacacho Rhythm 1953

Denmark's Bourbon Genius 1950

Hide-A-Way's Wild Country 1970

Oman's Desdemona Denmark 1953

CH Wing Commander 1943

Private Contract 1947

The Contract's Commander 1957

Callaway's Johnny Gillen 1959

CH Will Shriver 1966

Chief of Greystone 1962

Attache 1972

CH Yorktown 1964

Flight Time 1962

*Talent Town 1978

New Yorker 1970

Fountain of Youth 1972

*Chubasco 1977

Wing's Fleet Admiral 1959

*CH Superior Odds 1967

Grape Tree's Fox 1966

Genius Better Bourbon 1951 (a.k.a. Chief of Choice)

Genius Mountain Bourbon 1957

Lloyd's Genius Bourbon Prophet 1957

Greenway Commander 1964

Mountain Highland Memories 1971

Shoreacres Anacacho Genius 1949

Hide-A-Way's Firefly Supreme 1959

*Fire Lane 1964

Hide-A-Way's Evening Fire 1968

CH Valley View Supreme 1952

Supreme Spirit 1967

Longview's Supreme 1960

American Spirit 1971

High Rise Spirit 1973

I'm Super 1976

Status Symbol 1960

CH Night Prowler 1972

The Rambler 1950

Royal Rambler 1956

CH Irish American 1964

Super Supreme 1968

Supreme Sultan 1966

*Champagne Fizz 1973

*Sultan's Santana 1970

*Worthy Son 1973

Bourbon Chief

Harrison Chief

Chester Peavine

"The Boss," Harrison Chief was never raced but for many years was a top performer in the "harness rings" of the day, which were akin to fine harness classes but required more speed.

Cromwell and W. H. Wilson, who had developed Abdallah Park at Cynthiana, were apparently good friends. Abdallah Park was one of America's premier trotting tracks until Lexington's Red Mile came to the fore in the 1880s under Wilson's direction. W. H. Wilson's pride and joy was the great harness mare, Lady DeJarnette. Paired with Harrison Chief, they were unbeatable.

Harrison Chief was called by Herbert Krum, "Probably the most perfectly gaited trotting horse that ever wore leather. His action of both knee and hock was extreme. He never wore a boot and was never known to touch himself anywhere. No horse against which he ever contested could compare with him in the manner in which he could get into his highest rate of speed. Harrison Chief was shown for eight years, beginning as a suckling, and was defeated only four times." He was shipped by rail only a few times and was usually driven to the horse shows.

His most notable defeat came at Lexington, when he was tied second to Mambrino King, known worldwide as the handsomest horse in the world. Krum wrote that many horsemen considered the verdict unjust: "Although Mambrino King was a horse of incomparable beauty when standing, the harness covered him up, and in speed and action Harrison Chief made him look like a cart horse."

Harrison Chief was first used at stud as a three-year-old, and he made 21 seasons at Cromwell's Locust Grove Breeding Farm in Cynthiana, Kentucky. James Cromwell said "The Boss" was an immediate success, that several outstanding geldings came from his first crop of 15 or 20 foals.

It was estimated that he sired an average of fifty foals a year for a total of more than 1,000 sons and daughters. Cromwell did not consider Harrison Chief a Saddle Horse and would take issue with those who did. He was a registered trotter, as were many of his get, but for the most part these horses were not race horses but were used as stylish driving animals.

The best registered sons of Harrison Chief were Bourbon Chief, the sire of Bourbon King, and Wilson's King, sire of Annie C., the dam of Bourbon King. Bourbon Chief was also the sire of Emily, shown by General John B. Castleman to win the five gaited mare class at the Chicago World's Fair of 1893. This did much to popularize Chief breeding. Bracken Chief and Harrison Chief, Jr., were also good sires.

His most famous daughter was Lou Chief, owned by John T. Hughes and remembered for her famous show ring duels with Rex McDonald.

Harrison Chief died in 1896, and he was said to have been buried next to Gaines Denmark. He was recognized as a great sire during his lifetime, but his tremendous continuing impact on the American Saddlebred became obvious when CH Wing Commander came on the show scene.

Rex McDonald

Bourbon King

33

Tom Hal

Foundation Sires

Davy Crockett

Harrison Chief has now been elevated to the status he justly deserves, that of Foundation Sire. James Cromwell would have been pleased that "The Boss" now shares laurels with Denmark.

In addition to Denmark F.S. and Harrison Chief F.S., the original foundation sires were: Brinker's Drennon, Sam Booker, John Dillard, Tom Hal, Coleman's Eureka, Van Meter's Waxy, Cabell's Lexington, Copperbottom, Stump the Dealer, Texas, Prince Albert, Peters' Halcorn, Varnon's Roebuck, Davy Crockett and Pat Cleburne.

These stallions were undoubtedly considered great sires in their day, and each probably helped to establish the breed. The contributions of Brinker's Drennon, Varnon's Roebuck, Texas, Van Meter's Waxy, Prince Albert, John Dillard, and Stump the Dealer have been lost to the sands of time.

Davy Crockett, Copperbottom, and Tom Hal were very important in that they were pacing horses brought to Kentucky from Canada, a repository of the old Naragansett blood.

Davy Crockett 3236 was brought to Woodford County, Kentucky, and went to Eminence, Kentucky, in 1840 where he made four seasons at stud. He died in 1845 or 1846. He has no known pedigree. Davy Crockett was said to be unbeaten in races at the pace and was described as seal brown in color with large, yellow eyes. He was the sire of Brinker's Drennon and grandsire of the dam of Pat Cleburne.

Copperbottom 1601, pedigree unknown, was imported about 1812. He was described as being roan colored with a copper tinge, and he could trot, pace, fox trot, and do the running walk. Copperbottom sired the dam of Bald Stockings by Tom Hal and the second dam of Cabell's Lexington.

Tom Hal 3237 was a blue roan horse foaled in 1802 in Canada and died in Kentucky in 1843. A great breeding horse, he founded the Hal family of Standardbred pacers in Tennessee, the Blue Bull family of pacers in Indiana, and the Tom Hall Saddlebreds in Kentucky. His son Bald Stockings sired Queen 58, the dam of Diamond Denmark, Latham's Denmark, Jewel Denmark, and King William.

Coleman's Eureka 3238 was Morgan-bred on the top of his pedigree, Thoroughbred on the bottom. He was a dark chestnut stallion foaled in 1864 and died in 1898. He was a top five gaited show horse of his day.

Peters' Halcorn 3241 was Thoroughbred on his sire's side, but his dam was unknown. Foaled in 1835, he was described as bay with a white star and feet, and very fine. He died in 1856, leaving a legacy of fine Saddle Horses.

Pat Cleburne 3242 was a 16 hand grey horse sired by a Thoroughbred. His dam was by Skinner's Joe by Davy Crockett. He was foaled in 1864 in Kentucky and went to Missouri where he spent his days in the St. Joseph area. He was known to have sired gold and dun colored horses.

Copper Bottom

Coleman's Eureka

Pat Cleburne

35

Gaines' Denmark

Confederate Raid

*Gaines' Denmark
Recovered*

Other stallions were very important to the breed but were not recognized as foundation sires. The most important of these were:

Gaines' Denmark 58 by Denmark F.S. and out of the Stevenson Mare by Cockspur. Gaines' Denmark was bred by W. V. Cromwell of Lexington and foaled in 1851. A beautiful black stallion, he was sold for a record $1,000.00 to Edward P. Gaines, Georgetown, Kentucky in 1854. He was a terrific five gaited show horse and sire. He was sold to Willis Jones of Woodford County, Kentucky, in 1860. Jones also owned the great trotting stallion Mambrino Chief who died in the spring of 1862. Gaines' Denmark continued to show until Jones entered the Confederate Army that October. Gaines' Denmark was sent to Woodburn Farm, owned by R. A. Alexander, a British citizen. It was thought horses there would be safe from marauders, but Woodburn Farm was raided several times. Gaines' Denmark was probably taken by General John Hunt Morgan's men on his Ohio raid in 1863 and was among the horses which escaped capture by Union troops.

Willis Jones apparently saw the horse when Morgan's men (who escaped), came to Abingdon, Virginia. Jones recovered the horse and sent him back to Woodburn Farm where he stood the seasons of 1864 and 1865. Jones was killed in the fighting near Richmond, Virginia, in late 1864.

Gaines' Denmark was sold to James W. Cromwell, Cynthiana, Kentucky, in 1865 and died there in 1866. James Cromwell was the cousin of

W. V. Cromwell. James Cromwell later bred and owned Harrison Chief F.S., and both Gaines' Denmark and Harrison Chief F.S. died on the same farm.

A notation in Volume I of the American Saddlebred Registry calls Gaines' Denmark "probably the greatest progenitor of Saddle Horses that ever lived. What Hambletonian 10 was to trotters, Gaines' Denmark was to Saddlers."

Cockspur was foaled in 1837 in Virginia. His sire, Cock Robin, was of Thoroughbred lineage, being by a son of Janus and out of a daughter of Celer. Cockspur's dam was by the Thoroughbred Hotspur, and his second dam a roan saddle mare said to be very fast at the rack. Cockspur was killed by a train in 1864 in Illinois where he had been taken from Missouri for safety during the Civil War. Cockspur sired the dam of Gaines' Denmark, and his blood was important in many other Saddle Horses in Kentucky and Missouri.

Peavine 85 was by the Morgan-bred stallion Rattler, and his dam was Thoroughbred. He was foaled near Lawrenceburg, Kentucky, in 1863 and died near Richmond, Kentucky, in 1887. He was an outstanding show horse in harness and could also rack under saddle. His daughters were among the greatest producing mares of all time.

Some of the great foundation mares of the Saddlebred were the Stevenson Mare, the Saltram Mare, Betsey Harrison, Pekina, Lute Boyd, Lucy Mack, Daisy 2nd, Queen 48, and Annie C.

John B. Castleman on Carolina

Cockspur foaled

Great Foundation Mares

King's Sport by Bourbon King

*Breeding stallion owned by Winganeek Farm,
Lexington, Kentucky (Clara Peck, heiress
to Woolworth fortune). Stood at stud in the
1930s. This painting was used for many years
by the American Saddlebred Horse Association
as a depiction of the "ideal Saddlebred."*

CONFORMATION

ince the beginning of time, a certain type of horse has been fixed in the mind's eye of man: a proud, high-stepping horse with arched neck and flaring nostrils. Ancient Greek, Roman, and Oriental art depicts this animal vividly. This horse is alive today in the American Saddlebred.

American Saddlebreds range in height from 15 to 17 hands (a hand is four inches) with an average size of about 15.3 hands or 63 inches. They weigh from 1,000 to 1,200 pounds.

Saddlebreds come in many colors because registration is based strictly on pedigree with no color restrictions. The primary color is chestnut, varying from a dark liver color to red or nearly gold. Bay is found frequently as are brown, black and grey. A number of Saddlebreds are golden with white manes and tails (true palominos), and there are many spotted Saddlebreds with chestnut, black or bay, mixed with white. Varying shades of roan are seen.

Several physical characteristics make Saddlebreds unique. They differ from most other breeds in the head and neck, the feet and legs, and the top line:

According to the authoritative U. S. text, *Modern Breeds of Livestock* by Briggs, "Perhaps the most striking portion of the American Saddlebred Horse is its head and neck. The neck is long and has considerable arch.

"The head of the American Saddlebred is extremely well-proportioned and refined in appearance; the ears are small and placed at the top of the head, and the throatlatch is characteristically clean. Everything about the head and eye suggests quality, refinement and intelligence.

"Even the casual observer notices the long, sloping pasterns and the well shaped foot of the Saddlebred. The long pastern gives a spring to the stride which is not possible in horses with short stubby pasterns; this makes the Saddlebred very comfortable to ride.

"The top line of the Saddlebred has a long, level croup, a short strong coupling and back and a high, well-defined withers. In contrast to other light horses, the withers should be well above the height of the hips. The body of the Saddlebred is more rounding than that found on most other types and results from a well-sprung but shallow rib.

"The overall appearance of the American Saddlebred Horse is one of great refinement, smoothness, and good proportions, presenting a beautiful overall picture."

Longevity and a long, useful life are characteristics of the breed. CH Imperator won the World's Champion Five Gaited Gelding title at age 14. It is not unusual for stallions and broodmares to have a reproductive life well into their 20s.

The conformation of the American Saddlebred enables him to perform well in all equine events, and from its early ancestors the breed has inherited the ability to learn to do the elegant stepping pace and the flashy, speedy rack.

Perhaps the most distinguishing trait of the American Saddlebred horse is high intelligence. Most American Saddlebreds seem to want to please, are happy and courageous horses. Extremely alert and curious they possess that indescribable quality — personality, making them people-oriented and endearing them to their owners and admirers.

Head: Well-shaped with large, wide-set, expressive eyes, gracefully-hooked ears set close together on top of the head and carried alertly; a straight face line with a relatively fine muzzle, large nostrils, and a clean, smooth jaw line.

Neck: Long, arched and well-flexed at the poll, with a fine, clean throatlatch.

Shoulders: Deep and sloping.

Feet: Good and sound, open at the heel, neither toed-in nor toed-out.

THE IDEAL SADDLEBRED

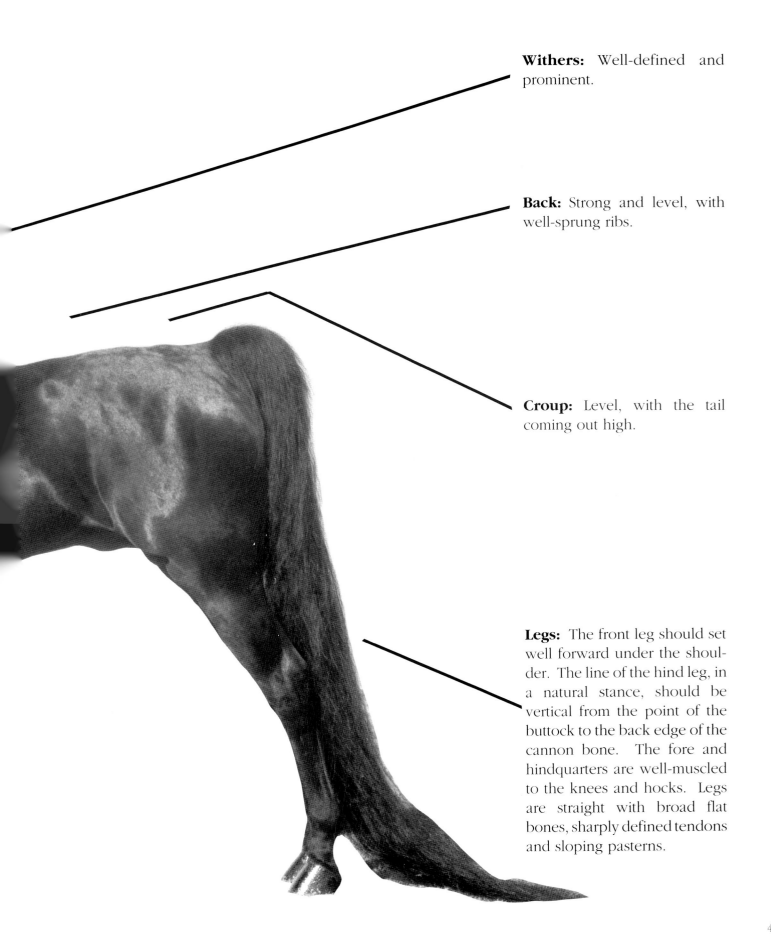

Withers: Well-defined and prominent.

Back: Strong and level, with well-sprung ribs.

Croup: Level, with the tail coming out high.

Legs: The front leg should set well forward under the shoulder. The line of the hind leg, in a natural stance, should be vertical from the point of the buttock to the back edge of the cannon bone. The fore and hindquarters are well-muscled to the knees and hocks. Legs are straight with broad flat bones, sharply defined tendons and sloping pasterns.

American Saddlebred Horse Association Headquarters, Lexington, Kentucky

THE SADDLEBRED ASSOCIATION

hen the American Saddlebred Horse Association was founded April 8, 1891 in Louisville, Kentucky, it became the first such organization for an American breed of horse.

A registry for "Saddle Horses" had first been proposed shortly after the Civil War, but no action was taken until the 1880s when a group of breeders from Missouri and other Midwestern states began sending proposed registrations to Charles F. Mills in Springfield, Illinois.

This caught the attention of Kentuckians who had been raising thouands of Saddle Horses as a cash crop since the early 1800s.

General John B. Castleman of Louisville journeyed to Mexico, Missouri, early in 1891 to meet with breeders and encourage formation of Saddle Horse Association. His efforts were favorably received.

About 100 Saddlebred breeders from Kentucky, Missouri, Illinois, Tennessee and Texas met on April 8, 1891 and the National Saddle-Horse Breeders' Association was organized.

The association's first registry volume was published in 1892.

Eighteen states were represented in the first volume, plus the province of Quebec.

In 1899, the name of the organization was changed to the American Saddle Horse Breeders' Association. Denmark was designated the single foundation sire and henceforth referred to as Denmark F.S.

The most dramatic changes in the American Saddle Horse Breeders Association since the early days began in 1980 with the election of James Aikman of Indianapolis as president.

The corporate structure of the organization was altered to incorporate an open membership policy. The name was changed to the American Saddlebred Horse Association, a name which describes the animal and encompasses not just breeders but all Saddlebred enthusiasts. Since then, the membership has grown to nearly 7,000.

ASHA headquarters in Louisville, Kentucky were moved in 1985 to the new American Saddle Horse Museum Building located in the Kentucky Horse Park in Lexington.

The American Saddlebred Horse Association is today custodian for the records of all registered American Saddlebreds.

Celebrating its centennial in 1991, the American Saddlebred Horse Association leads the way as the first breed association in America. ASHA is continually working to keep its light shining, and in 1991 it will sparkle even more brightly than ever.

Stonewall King

Stonewall King was a great sire from the 1920s until his death in 1949. His entire career at stud was spent near Columbia, Missouri. His owner, in the photograph, was Murray Cason.

THE BREED BUILDERS

hile the race track was the proving ground for Trotters and Thoroughbreds, the show ring was the proving ground for Saddle Horses, as Saddlebreds were known. Horse shows were usually a featured part of country fairs. The first Kentucky horse show on record was held near Lexington in 1816, and the first known show in Missouri was in 1833. It is probable that horse shows were held in the Colonies before then.

These shows were used by stock raisers to promote their horses; show ring winners would gain local notoriety. One must keep in mind that utility was a primary objective of horse breeders until World War I, and that one's own horse was a matter of great personal pride. The breeder of a show ring winner could be assured of the patronage of commercial horse buyers seeking saddle and harness horses for their clientele.

A number of the stallions originally designated as foundation sires, when the American Saddlebred Horse Association was established in 1891, had reputations as good show horses. Brinker's Drennon, foaled in 1843; Sam Booker; Harrison Chief, foaled in 1872; Cabell's Lexington, foaled 1863; and Coleman's Eureka, foaled in 1864, all established their prowess in the show ring.

Gaines' Denmark, an outstanding five gaited horse and truly the great progenitor of the Denmarks, was said to have been unbeaten throughout his show career in the 1850s.

Many Saddlebred-type horses became famous as the mounts of Civil War generals. The most famous was Robert E. Lee's Traveller, sired by the race horse Grey Eagle who is on so many Saddlebred pedigrees. Another great Thoroughbred, Lexington, was the sire of U. S. Grant's famous charger Cincinnati and also General Sherman's horse Lexington.

General George Meade, commander of Union forces at Gettysburg, rode a bay gelding with a white face named Baldy. Baldy had no pedigree but was noted for his slow, comfortable rack. Stonewall Jackson's horse Little Sorrell also possessed the easy gaits. These horses added to the fame of the "Kentucky" Saddle Horse.

Following the Civil War, horsemen returned to the show ring, and tremendous rivalries developed between Kentucky and Missouri. The ownership of famous horses swayed back and forth between the two states.

As communications improved, horses became folk heroes, rivaling athletes, soldiers, stars of theater and politicians. Mambrino LeGrand, Black Eagle and Sumpter Denmark were among the first famous post-Civil War performers.

Then came Montrose, the greatest and most

*King's Genius by Bourbon King
(at the trot)*

*World's Champion Five Gaited Stallion 1931,
1933, and 1934. Owned by Dixiana Farm,
Mary Gwyn Friers, Roger Selby, and Clifford
Mooers. Chester Caldwell up in painting.*

Anacacho Denmark

*A son of Edna May's King, is considered a great
breeding stallion. He is the only horse to have sired
all of the five gaited divisional winners and grand
champion at the World's Championship Horse Show
in the same year.*

exciting of those early horses. After much hoopla to clear a path through adoring crowds, Montrose would enter the ring at a full gallop, making one or two rounds before he settled down to work. During a show career of 14 years he defeated every horse shown against him. Montrose was sold 12 times and was the first Saddle Horse to command $5,000. He was champion at the St. Louis Fair, considered the leading show in America, at age 17.

Montrose

Artist, Black Squirrel, Chester Dare, and Rex Denmark, were notable contemporaries of Montrose in the show ring and the breeding shed.

Some famous early mares were General Castleman's Emily, winner at the 1893 World's Fair; Miss Rex, a beautiful grey mare shown by the black trainer Tom Bass; Lou Chief, Edna May and Hazel Dawn.

Although one of the basic criteria for the Saddlebred was the ability to perform the "saddle gaits," some horses were hard to rack. Although these "walk, trot and canter horses" were not popular in the heartland where the Saddle Horse was supreme, they were prized in the East. European instructors at many riding academies had no conception of the five gaited horse. A star at the first National Horse Show in Madison Square Garden, New York, in 1883, was the Saddlebred gelding Estes, winner of the three gaited class. He did much to popularize the breed in the East.

Emily, ridden by John B. Castleman

The trot was made as important as the saddle gaits in 1888, when horse show rules were changed to require Saddle Horses to perform at the trot. This changed breeding programs and the blood of "harness horses," primarily Standardbred (tracing to Messenger) and Morgan, was added to the breed.

Harness horses were very popular in all parts of the U. S., and some of the best known were Indian Chief, his daughter Lady DeJarnette, Wilson's King, Bourbon Chief, Mambrino King.

The first equine super star, Rex McDonald, was

Miss Rex

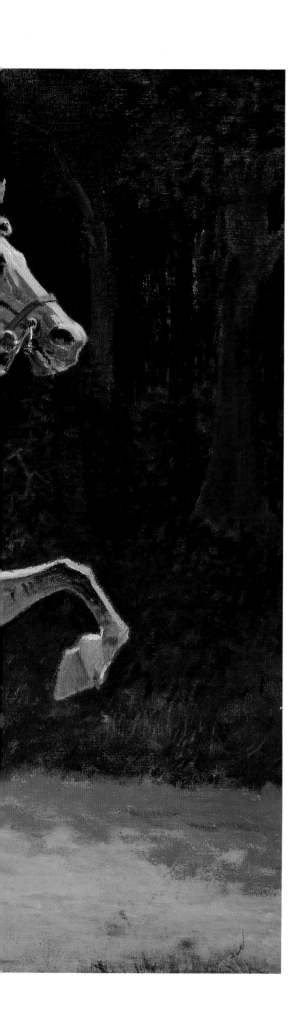

Sweetheart On Parade by Lee Rose McDonald (at the rack)

Considered one of the greatest five gaited mares. World's Grand Champion in 1931 and 1932. Owned by Mrs. W.P. Roth, Why Worry Farm, San Mateo, California. Trained and shown by Lonnie Hayden.

American Born

Guided by Love X Lena Jemison by Highland
Denmark
1921 - 1948
American Born was the nation's top rated sire four
times. He was owned by Robert Moreland,
Lexington, Kentucky, and Nawbeek Farm, Paoli,
Pennsylvania.

foaled in 1890 in Callaway County, Missouri. He captured the imagination of the American public and was admired by Presidents of the U.S.

The next super stars to emerge were Bourbon King, foaled in Kentucky in 1900, and the exquisitely beautiful three gaited gelding, Poetry of Motion, who made a command performance for the King of England at the Olympia horse show in London.

As the use of the automobile superceded the horse, the American Saddlebred was more and more relegated to the show ring. Competition was intense, the public enjoyed horse shows, and there were some great performers, but the next champion to grab public attention did not come along until 1925.

Chief of Longview, a great grandson of old Rex McDonald, won the five gaited championship at Kansas City's famed American Royal as a three-year-old. This was unheard of and set the public imagination on fire when it was announced he had been sold to Mrs. W. P. Roth of San Francisco for $25,000.

His contemporary in the three gaited division was a golden buckskin mare appropriately named Jonquil.

In 1931 Mrs. Roth's gorgeous grey mare Sweetheart on Parade hit the spotlight and lived up to her name, becoming America's equine sweetheart. At the same time, a chestnut mare named Roxie Highland was shown to three gaited championships by a striking blonde girl, Mary Gwyn Fiers.

Belle Le Rose and Oak Hill Chief were the next five gaited champions. America Beautiful dominated three gaited competition in the 1940s, and fine harness classes were made exciting by Vanity and Noble Kalarama.

Then, in 1946, a three-year-old stallion burst onto the show scene, CH Wing Commander. Owned by Dodge Stables, he was foaled near Detroit, Michigan, and then

Poetry of Motion

Chief of Longview

Jonquil

*Lady Jane by Independence Chief
(at the trot)*

*Five Gaited World's Grand Champion of
1939, shown by Harry Lathrop. Bred by
Longview Farm, Lee's Summit, Missouri.
Owned by Georgian Court Stables, Topeka,
Kansas, Pine Tree Farm, McHenry, Illinois,
and Crebilly Farm, Chester, Pennsylvania.
Trained by Garland Bradshaw, J. Miller
McAfee, Lloyd Teater, and Harry Lathrop. J.
Miller McAfee up in painting.*

CH The Lemon Drop Kid

Ch The Lemon Drop Kid was a unique fine harness horse who had the ability to generate great emotion in people. He seemed to interact with the audience and responded to applause. Jay Utz driving.

moved to Castleton Farm, Lexington, Kentucky. He was shown throughout his career by Earl Teater. CH Wing Commander was five gaited World's Grand Champion six times. He became famous and was even featured in Life Magazine.

CH Wing Commander was succeeded by another champion, CH Lady Carrigan. At the same time, the fine harness great CH The Lemon Drop Kid was publicly acclaimed. This light chestnut gelding had an extraordinarily dynamic personality which he was able to project to the audience. CH The Lemon Drop Kid was featured on the cover of *Sports Illustrated*, November, 1957.

CH Denmark's Daydream was an exceedingly beautiful mare who died tragically after twice winning the five gaited World's Championship at the Kentucky State Fair. She was succeeded by the powerful mare CH My-My, who went on to tie CH Wing Commander's record of six World's Grand Championships.

The epitome of the Saddlebred world, that hotly-contested title at Kentucky of five gaited World's Grand Champion, went into the 1970s with CH Yorktown, CH Surefire, CH Belle Elegant, CH Cora's Time, CH Will Shriver, and CH Mountain Highland Encore all providing excitement.

Then, in 1982, the reigning titleholder, a personality gelding with a great slow gait, CH Imperator, was upset by a young stallion grandson of CH Wing Commander named CH Sky Watch. These two great horses battled for supremacy throughout the decade. Horse lovers and railbirds could not recall when the show ring was so exciting.

CH Yorktown, ridden by Tom Moore

Recent Champions

CH Mountain Highland Encore, ridden by Chat Nichols

CH Wing Commander

CH Wing Commander is considered by many authorities to be the greatest five gaited stallion of modern times, winning six World's Grand Championships. He was owned by Dodge Stables and shown throughout his career by trainer Earl Teater. CH Wing Commander was shown fearlessly over nine years (1946-1954) making appearances in eleven states. He was beaten only twice, both times by the aged mare Daneshall's Easter Parade, when he was just four years old. CH Wing Commander went on to have an outstanding career at stud.

CH My - My

CH My-My is the only mare to have won the World's Championship six times, tying CH Wing Commander's record. She was trained and shown by Frank Bradshaw, Georgetown, Kentucky. CH My-My was a daughter of Daneshall's Easter Parade.

Belle Reve Farm, Versailles, Kentucky.

SADDLEBRED FARMS

The Saddlebred Horse, for all its beauty and elegance, has as its foundation a long history of utility. This was a horse to be found not just on large, fancy Saddlebred farms, but on thousands of small family farms all over the midwest and south. The Saddlebred was an integral part of many a family's work and daily life. So, especially in the early days, there was no such thing as a "typical" Saddlebred horse farm.

But even in the early 19th century there were Saddlebred farms especially dedicated to the breeding and development of Saddlebred horses. From these showcase farms came many of the breed-building champions of the past century. No recounting of Saddlebred history would be complete without mentioning Kalarama Farm or Allie Jones and Sons or Blythewood or Arthur Simmons Stable or Dodge Stables or Anacacho Ranch. These historic farms and dozens of others distinguished themselves by generations of success and leadership in the development of Saddlebreds.

The big farms are merely the most visible examples of a common enthusiasm held by many thousands of small-family and single-horse owners and breeders throughout the country — the love of the Saddlebred horse and the lifestyle that training and riding the breed provides. Saddlebred people love the life of the farm and the rhythms of Saddlebred care, training, grooming and show preparation. It is a life of extraordinary intimacy with the horse,more so than virtually any other breed. Saddlebred ownership is very often a family affair, with everyone pitching in and contributing to some aspect of life on the farm or in the stable.

The Ball Brothers Farm near Versailles, Kentucky was a famous breeding farm in the early 1900s. Montgomery Chief, in the painting above with the Ball Brothers, dominated the Kentucky Saddlebred scene.

*At Oak Hill Farm in Harrodsburg, Kentucky, grave stones mark the burial sites
of two five-gaited world's champions, Oak Hill Chief and CH Yorktown.*

*Castleton Farm, Lexington, Kentucky, was the home
of many world's champions, including six-time five-
gaited grand champion, CH Wing Commander.*

Overleaf; Undulata Farm, Shelbyville, Kentucky

*The memorabilia of past triumphs in the show ring
adorn the walls of many Saddlebred barns and offices.
These (above and below) are at Oak Hill Farm.*

Historic Castleton Farm trophy room, Lexington, Kentucky.

In preparing for daily exercise at Cismont Manor Farm, Keswick, Virginia, one passes the memories of great horses of the past that line the walls.

Grooming is an everyday activity in a Saddlebred barn.

An annual part of the Roanoke Horse Show is the Bent Tree Farm lawn party.

Bent Tree Farm, Shawsville, Virginia.

Jack Noble Stable, Versailles, Kentucky.

(Both above) El Milagro Farm, Salinas, California.

Early morning at Kalarama Farm, Springfield, Kentucky.

BREEDING

The American Saddlebred horse is a breed that from the beginning was adapted for special uses. Its valuable characteristics — easy-gaited movement, hardiness, sure-footedness, and gentility — were ideal for travelling long distances over rough terrain.

Those characteristics still define the unique conformation of the American Saddlebred. Over 100 years of breeding and registration, under the auspices of the American Saddlebred Horse Association, have yielded a uniformly sturdy, versatile, and beautiful horse, "recognized throughout the world," as General John B. Castleman said, "as distinctively an American horse."

As in other breeds of horse, the uniting of bloodlines to create desireable characteristics in the offspring is the challenge of breeding. Various breeders ascribe differing degrees of weight to sire pedigrees, dam pedigrees, individual past performances, physical characteristics and so on, hoping in the end to create a foal naturally inclined to perfect form in one discipline or another, be it the show ring, dressage, eventing, driving or pleasure. Sometimes it works, and sometimes it doesn't, but the quest for perfect breeding combinations is a driving force in the competitive world of Saddlebreds.

Generally, most breeders follow the tried-and-true wisdom of horse breeders everywhere — champion horses are built on solid foundations of generations of proven champion producers on both the stallion and broodmare sides. Although there are plenty of accidental successes, the get of champion bloodlines, when matched expertly, have demonstrated a consistency and reliability that are attractive to both beginning and veteran breeders.

Supreme Sultan, above left, Spring Valley's Deliverance, above right, and CH Will Shriver, below, are direct descendants of the two principal bloodlines in Saddlebreds, the Chiefs and the Denmarks.

Stallion Avenue, Finchville, Kentucky. Although some breeding is still done naturally, artificial insemination is now a common method of breeding American Saddlebreds.

*A groom makes a late-night inspection of a mare that is due to foal at
Ruxer Stables, Jasper, Indiana.*

Overleaf; Yearlings are left to play and exercise while they are growing.

Training a two-year-old horse in long lines, prior to being hitched to a cart at El Milagro Farm.

TRAINING

From birth, a Saddlebred foal will exhibit both a body type and an inherent "Saddlebred" way of going that shows its ancestry. But while bloodlines supply the building blocks of performance, it is the trainer who breaks the horse to the many facets of basic equine performance. For the most part, Saddlebreds receive an elementary training consisting of ground work with lunge lines and long lines before progressing to jog carts and mounted riders. These exercises give the horse an understanding of simple trainer commands such as stopping, starting, backing, and guiding. After the basics, a Saddlebred can be further trained to perform well in virtually any discipline of riding or driving, from dressage to the trails.

But the most evident public test of a trainer's skill is found in the show ring, where the years of training and work are appraised by the critical eyes of judges.

The gaits of the Saddlebred horse in the show ring are carefully developed and strengthened, and the trainer is the teacher. As with human beings, there are subtleties to the education of young horses that make each case to some degree unique. A veteran trainer will recognize the special qualities of his horse, and will lead the horse gently to the customized work he has to do.

Through a wide variety of techniques, unique to each trainer and so numerous that there are whole books devoted to the subject, the Saddlebred can be taught the movements and requirements of each gait until proficiency is reached.

Championship form is always the result of both the horse's inherent abilities and the skilfullness and dedication of a good trainer.

*An enclosed ring is often, but not always, used when training
horses with long lines.*

Horses can be introduced gently to a rider's weight by first lying across the saddle before actually sitting astride.

The horse gradually becomes accustomed to the sensation of a rider's weight.

Experienced horses are also exercised with long lines so that the trainer can watch the horse's movements from the ground. This training session takes place at Premier Stables, Simpsonville, Kentucky.

A jog cart is nearly always a part of a Saddlebred's training. This light-weight wheeled vehicle is pulled by the Saddlebred, guided by the horseman seated behind. It is used to develop general fitness and stamina. Jogging is alternated with riding in the training schedule.

THE GAITS

Almost all horses have the innate ability to perform the walk, trot, and canter. But Saddlebreds have inherited the aptitude to learn the lateral gaits, the slow gait and the rack, from their forebears, the Naragansett pacers.

Each gait has its own performance criteria, but all require beauty of movement, symmetry, balance, and the natural action for which Saddlebreds are famous.

The Walk is a springy, collected, four-beat gait that is called for between other gaits in the show ring.

The Trot is a two-beat, diagonal gait in which the front foot and opposite hind foot leave the ground in unison and land simultaneously. Show ring judges look for an even, balanced trot, high action with good shoulder movement, and flexing hocks working close together.

The Canter is a relatively slow gallop, a three-beat gait comfortable for horse and rider, performed with collection and control. Two diagonal legs are paired and move forward and back together. The unpaired legs act independently, creating the three-beat cadence. One foreleg leads, followed by the diagonal hind.

The Slow Gait is a four-beat gait performed by the five gaited horse and is sometimes called a "stepping pace." Two legs on the same side move simultaneously, but the hind foot contacts the ground slightly before the front foot in a four beat cadence. This gait is executed slowly, emphasizing precision and form and is very comfortable to ride.

The Rack is a four beat gait like the slow gait in that each foot contacts the ground separately and is comfortable for the rider. However, this gait is highly animated, performed with great action and speed while maintaining proper form.

THE TROT

In the Trot, the Saddlebred's diagonal pair of feet strike the ground at the same time, followed by the remaining diagonal pair. In the picture above, the horse is shown on his left diagonal (left front and right hind legs are raised).

In this transition to the right diagonal, all four of the horse's feet are off the ground.

THE RACK

The Rack is a four-beat gait in which only one of the horse's feet meets the ground at a time in equal, separate intervals. Above, the horse is shown with his right front leg on the ground.

A moment later, the right front leg is just about to push off as the left rear leg prepares to reach the ground.

Completing the transition, the horse is now on its right diagonal (right front and left hind legs are raised).

Quarter boots are part of a Saddlebred's inventory of athletic equipment. They are used to prevent an injury in the unlikely event of overstriding. These are used only on five gaited horses.

The weight now transfers to the left rear leg as it touches the ground, the left front leg preparing to meet the ground next.

The left foot is now on the ground, with the left hind preparing to touch the ground.

A full show bridle on a five-gaited contender.

Harness headstall.

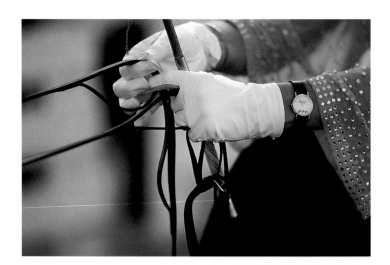

Bits of all types are a means by which riders communicate riding commands to their horses. Show bridles are customized for individual horses, and usually consist of a jointed snaffle bit which guides and steadies the horse, or raises its head into position, and a curb bit which may be used for control and to fine-tune or "set" the head position.

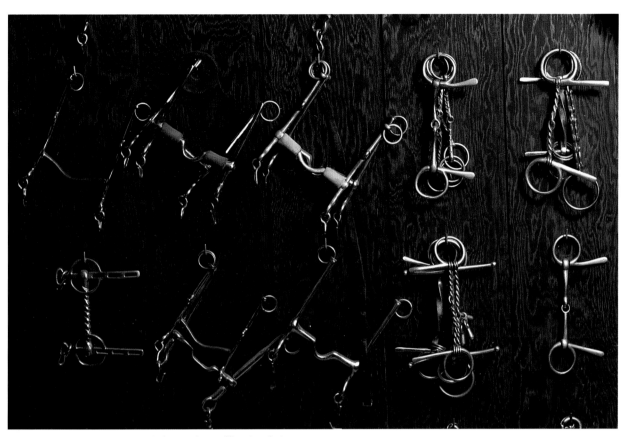

A display of curb bits (left) and snaffles (right).

A western curb bit.

A full show bridle on a three-gaited horse.

Horse's shoes being reset at Jack Nevitt Stables.

A rolled toe shoe is most commonly used on five-gaited horses.

As a rule, Saddlebreds have healthy, sound feet. Proper shoeing of a horse helps maintain that natural soundness.

A Saddlebred's shoe is an extension of his natural foot, following the angle of the hoof wall to the ground, giving the horse more surface to stand on. It is, in essence, a custom shoe, with pads in place for cushioning and shock absorption. These shoes are very comfortable for the horse, and as such can greatly improve performance.

The angle of the foot is important to the horse's proper movement and balance.

A temporary dressing is often used to enhance the color of the hoof for the show ring.

The stylish tail carriage of some show Saddlebreds is achieved by the use of the "tail set", a light harness with a padded crupper to elevate the tail. To enable the horse to wear a set comfortably while in its stall, a simple surgical procedure (a small incision in the ventral tail muscles) is sometimes performed to free the tail to move in all directions. The well-cared-for incision quickly heals, and full use of the tail is retained.

A set tail.

A natural tail.

The Tattersalls Summer Sale, one of three Tattersalls auctions per year, is the country's largest public Saddlebred sale. The summer auction is held in July at the same time as the Junior League Horse Show in Lexington, Kentucky.

SALES

As far back as the Colonial era, the sale of horses in America was often an occasion for public congregation, with social, as well as economic, implications. Today, there are several large sales per year where Saddlebred owners, buyers, and breeders still gather to buy and sell horses, and talk shop.

These public sales may be conducted by an equine sales firm such as Tattersalls, or they may be organized by large farms such as Kalarama. Further, at various times of the year a farm may elect to hold a dispersal sale of its Saddlebred stock, to realign with a new bloodline or to relieve an overstock situation.

For over one hundred years the ASHA has been registering Saddlebred horses; it is the oldest breed registry in the United States. With this long history of bloodlines and past performances to study, Saddlebred buyers often come to sales looking for one particular type of horse, one sire line, or some specialized pedigree.

Unlike their Thoroughbred counterparts who see only a horse's conformation, Saddlebred buyers at sales meetings get to watch many of the sale horses perform under saddle or in harness. The bidding progresses as the horse moves through his program of gaits, which adds an element of entertainment, performance and skillful observation to the auction.

Professionals may look for young horses with promise; they may look for finished horses for the show ring; or they may be buying for a particular owner with a specific use in mind. Amateur owners also have a place in Saddlebred sales, often finding good horses at acceptable prices for general purposes.

The Saddlebred is prized among the Amish as a buggy horse because of its good looks and harness skills. This auction in the New Holland sales barn is in historic Lancaster County, Pennsylvania.

Kalarama Farm is one of several farms that sell their horses annually at a private auction.

*The World's Championship Horse Show is held at the Kentucky
State Fair, Louisville, Kentucky.*

SHOWS

By far the majority of Saddlebred horses in the U.S. are used for purposes other than competitive Saddlebred shows. But the Saddlebred industry finds its truly shining moments in the color, pageantry, tradition, excitement, glamor, and athleticism of the big shows that are held annually at sites across the country. For world-class Saddlebreds, the big shows are the major leagues of the Saddlebred world.

At high levels such as this, championship contenders will all exhibit great "quality" in every phase of the game — conformation, movement, manners, discipline, form, speed and of course, an indefinable winning charisma. And when the best of the best compete in head-to-head showdowns, Saddlebred fans get their biggest thrills of the year.

Old hands can tell of the stirring duels they have witnessed in the show rings of the past — Sweetheart on Parade vs. Belle Le Rose and King's Genius, CH Wing Commander vs. The Replica, CH My-My vs. The Contender. These brilliant performances and many others produce the legends and lore of the sport that intrigue even the casual Saddlebred fan.

On a more practical level, the major shows present a way for the industry to compare one horse to another, or one pedigree to another, or one type to another, and in this way find clues to the development of better horses.

Of course, the highest levels of Saddlebred competition involve only a small percentage of owners, trainers and riders. For the majority of competition-minded Saddlebred owners, the local and regional horse shows and county fairs provide a good test of skill and horsemanship without putting extreme pressure on anyone. The smaller shows are family-oriented affairs, where the emphasis is no less on winning, but where the stakes are less and costs are more manageable.

Overleaf; The Iowa State Fair, Des Moines.

There are many popular Saddlebred horse shows around the country,
like this one at the Deerfield Fair, Deerfield, New Hampshire.

Stall front, California.

Action at a county fair.

Spectators at ringside.

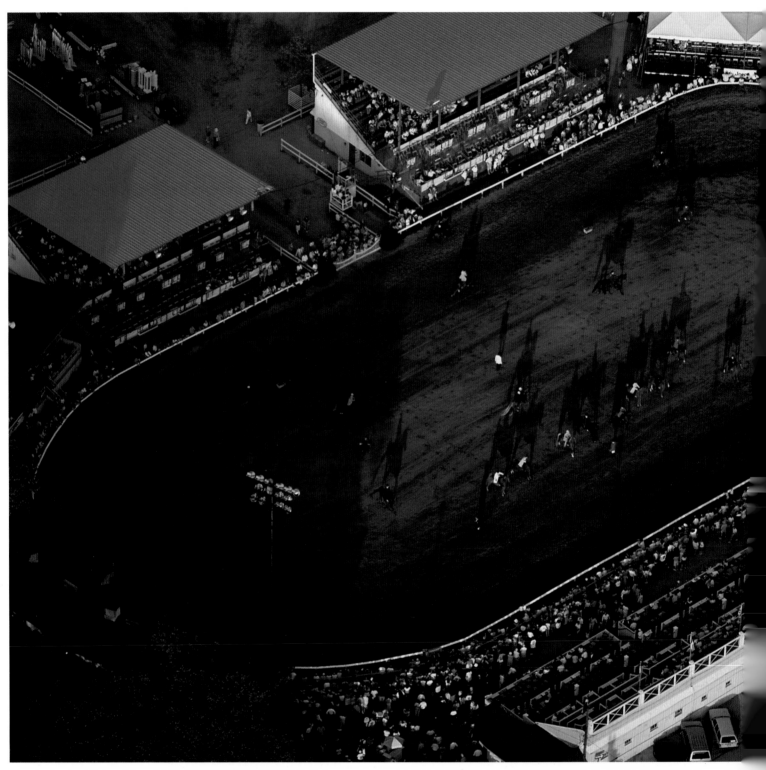

*The Devon Horse Show, one of the oldest shows in the country,
at Devon, Pennsylvania.*

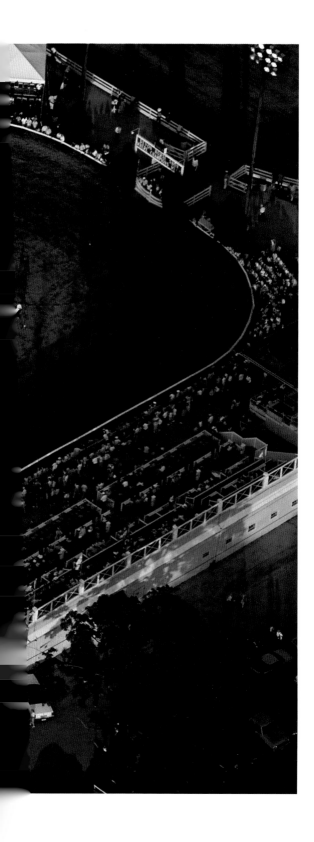

The National Pleasure Championship, Springfield, Illinois.

The Del Mar Charity Horse Show, Del Mar, California.

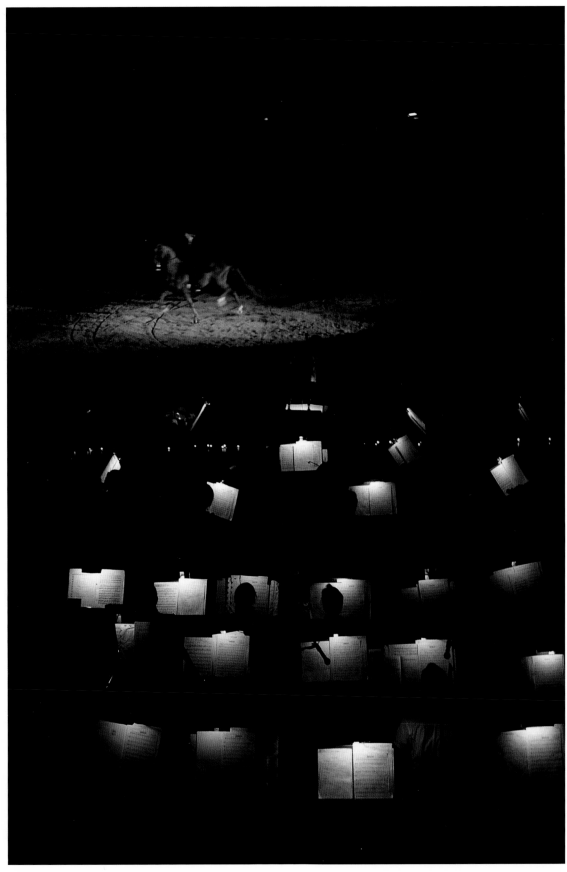

*A new and exciting performance synchronizes the music of a symphony orchestra
and the movement of the horse in a night of entertainment, Roanoke, Virginia.*

A party for the Roanoke, Virginia "Music in Motion" event.

The Kentucky State Fair.

Shively Stable, Kentucky State Fair.

Crabtree Stable, Kentucky State Fair.

Mystery Hill Stable, American Royal, Kansas City, Missouri.

Stall and tack room decorations, American Royal .

This trophy is given to the winner of the Five Gaited World's Grand Championship.

Competing at the rack shows the speed of the Saddlebred while maintaining form and style.

The world champion, CH Sky Watch, with Mitchell Clark riding, performs at a trot. The five gaited horse is shown with a full mane and tail.

Five gaited horses perform two gaits in addition to the walk, trot and canter — the slow gait and the rack, going both ways in the ring.

This class is considered by many to be the most exciting and spectacular in any show because of the speed and strength exhibited by these athletic horses. In fact, protective boots are worn on the front feet to prevent possible injury from the back feet when moving fast.

While sometimes deemed less fine than three gaited horses, the five gaited horses must be exceptionally fit and sound in order to compete.

Five gaited horses display full manes and tails, and a braided ribbon is added at the foretop and mane.

Overleaf: CH Imperator winning the Five Gaited World's Championship at the Kentucky State Fair, with Don Harris riding.

Warming up in the stable area in preparation for the show ring.

Three gaited horses perform the walk, trot and canter both ways in the show ring.

These gaits are collected, with the emphasis on animation and precision. Beauty, brilliance, elegance, refinement, expression and high action are all part of a winning performance.

Three gaited horses are distinguished from five gaited competitors by their appearance in the ring — the mane and the dock of the tail are clipped (roached) to accentuate the quality of the three gaited horse's appearance.

The Three Gaited Pony Class (mares and geldings 14.2 hands and under).

The Three Gaited Junior Exhibitor Class.

The view upon entering the show ring. This Saddlebred's head and neck show refinement and proud carriage.

CH Sultan's Starina being judged for conformation in the Three Gaited World's Championship.

The Fine Harness Class, Devon Horse Show, near Philadelphia, Pennsylvania.

*Preparing for the class at The Lexington Junior League Horse Show,
Lexington, Kentucky.*

Fine harness horses perform two gaits, the walk and the trot, going
both ways in the ring.

The horse does an animated, springy walk in which speed is not a
factor. Good performers are beautiful, fine, alert and airy. They are
penalized for cantering ("breaking").

Fine harness horses have full manes and tails, and boots are worn
on the front feet, not so much for protection as for tradition and good
appearance.

Competitor entering the Ladies Class, Kentucky State Fair.

Fine Harness World's Grand Championship, Kentucky State Fair.

Model Class, International Pleasure Championships, Springfield, Illinois.

A Pleasure Horse should create the impression that it is an agreeable mount to ride, either in the ring or on the trail. As such it shows typical Saddlebred qualities — style, quality, presence, a suitable conformation, and prompt, comfortable gaits. Judges look for a true, flat walk, and smooth transitions between gaits.

Three gaited, five gaited and Driving Pleasure Horses have full manes and tails, and wear boots only in five gaited events.

Spring Premier Horse Show, Lexington, Kentucky.

Three Gaited Pleasure division, Devon Horse Show.

Weanling Futurity Class, The National Horse Show, at the Meadowlands, New Jersey.

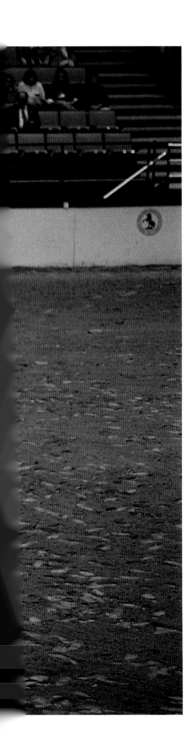

Iowa State Fair, Des Moines, Iowa.

In Hand classes offer breeders of Saddlebreds the opportunity to showcase their young horses and to compete for generous prize money in Futurity classes and Breeders Stakes.

Horses are led into the ring, one at a time, showing at the trot and are judged according to standards for the ideal American Saddlebred. Judges will consider how the youngster moves "on the line" and the natural action shown. Two people handle the horse, one leading and one at the rear to help keep the animal moving in a straight line.

Many of these young Saddlebreds are in the ring for the first time and offer the spectator an exciting sneak preview of the next generation of show horses.

*William Shatner Western Pleasure qualifying class at the Iowa State
Fair Horse Show.*

Saddlebreds show in Western Pleasure classes
with a western saddle and bridle at a flat walk, slow
trot, and a lope (a slow canter). The horse should
work on a loose rein and show good manners.
Riders wear typical western dress.

Like the Pleasure Horse division in general, the
Western Pleasure divisions are becoming more
popular every year.

Del Mar Charity Horse Show, Del Mar, California.

Getting ready to perform. Showmanship and appearance are always important to judges.

Riders congregate in the warm-up area just prior to entering the show ring.

Performing in the class. The rider enters the ring at the trot, is judged at the walk, trot and canter, moving both ways in the ring.

Equitation involves the development of the broad spectrum of riding skills known simply as horsemanship. It is the learning and perfecting of both the physical side of riding — balance, hand control, body position, foot position, stamina, strength — and the mental side, which involves grace, poise, intellect and "feel" that is necessary for exacting the maximum possible performance from a horse.

Saddlebreds are the most desired and most commonly used horses in the world for "Saddle Seat" equitation for several reasons:

• Their conformation, featuring high head carriage and level topline create an excellent saddle seat position.

• The Saddlebred moves in a balanced, precise, and stylish way that is a perfect complement to the rider.

• Saddlebreds are responsive, intelligent, well mannered and game, all qualities that maximize the skills of the rider.

Being judged in the lineup...

Waiting for results...

She learns that she has won her class...

She picks up the blue ribbon...

Rider and trainer celebrate the win.

Training Level Dressage at the Kentucky Horse Park.

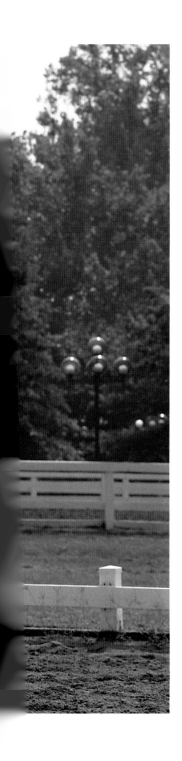

DRESSAGE

Prix St. Georges Level formal attire.

Saddlebreds, while not traditionally known as dressage horses, show remarkable ability in this discipline.

Long before "classical dressage" became popular in the U.S., Saddlebreds were stars of "high school" classes, which were held from the 1870s until after World War I. Some horses such as Belle Beach, Columbus, and Limestone Belle became nationally famous.

Saddlebreds are intelligent and even tempered, taking nicely to the long years of training necessary to perform the intricate maneuvers of classical dressage. Further, its conformation, with natural hock action and athletic shoulder motion, lends itself beautifully to dressage work. Add this to the horse's natural beauty and elegance, and the Saddlebred shows not only trainability but suitability for international-level dressage.

Saddlebred horses often compete in Hunter/Jumper shows like this one near Boston, Massachusetts.

JUMPING AND EVENTING

For equine events such as stadium jumping, cross-country, dressage, and others that require jumping ability, the Saddlebred can be the perfect mount. Physically, the horse presents an athletic build, with strength in the hips for power in the jumps. Plus, the horse is naturally limber and folds easily, creating a graceful, smooth line over obstacles.

Best of all, Saddlebreds bring a hard-working, trusting and willing attitude to jumping, giving a rider great confidence and producing great rapport and compatibility for the horse/rider team.

A Park Drag with a four-in-hand matched Saddlebred team performs at the Strawberry Hill Steeplechase, Richmond, Virginia.

COACHING AND DRIVING

The Amish, Lancaster County, Pennsylvania.

Saddlebreds have always been superior harness horses. After all, they are descendants of the fine road horses that pulled the wagons and carriages of early America.

Saddlebreds are generally strong in the feet and rear quarters, making them good, fast, pulling animals. Drivers applaud their "perfect" mouths. Their superiority, however, derives from their good temperaments. They are "can-do" horses who show great willingness to please. These are important traits to carriage drivers for whom safety and trust are even more important than raw strength.

Saddlebreds are playing a substantial role in the coaching/driving scene which is enjoying a resurgence in popularity.

The versatile Saddlebred is a wonderful horse for riding on the trail as well as in the ring.

TRAIL AND ENDURANCE RIDING

Competitive trail ride, Salton, Massachusetts.

In a sport where the emphasis is on sturdiness, athleticism, and endurance, the Saddlebred makes an ideal mount. The Saddlebred is the ultimate in a "game" horse, trying to do everything asked of him. This alone makes him a worthy choice in these very tough competitions.

But the horse's physique makes him even better. He is a versatile horse, adaptable to the varying terrains one finds on endurance rides. His extended trot is well known for its ground-eating ability and is performed at the speed of other horses' canters. Overall, his athletic build lets him move more easily and well in this discipline than other less hardy and temperamental breeds.

Parade Horse division, St. Louis National Horse Show.

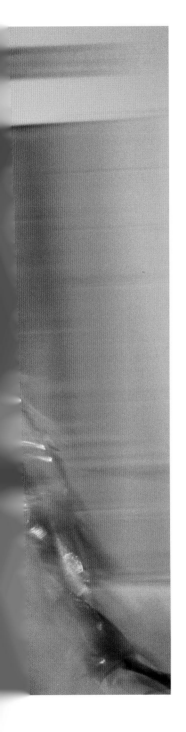

PARADE HORSES

A Parade Horse in Saddlebred terms can mean two things — a Saddlebred to be ridden in a parade, usually in fancy parade finery; and a Saddlebred in the "Parade Horse" division of a show.

Saddlebreds make wonderful parade horses, not only because they are pretty to look at and have a nice, showy gait that is perfect for parade pace, but also because they are calm and collected amid the noise and crowded quarters of a big public parade.

For the show ring, a Parade Horse should exhibit good Saddlebred traits and be of sufficient size to carry parade equipment easily, such as decorative saddles, breast plates and tapaderos. Parade horses are shown at an animated walk and a parade gait.

The Saddlebred is a popular horse among police departments because of its disposition and intelligence. This patrol is in Cleveland, Ohio.

POLICE HORSES

Horses add a unique dimension to law enforcement, and mounted police units are being maintained and added in many cities.

The Saddlebred presents a perfect combination of skills and personality for this specialized work. He can handle the often unpredictable physical aspects of the job — jumping, moving at speed, stamina — with ease. His innate good looks are important to the sometimes showy aspects of horse patrol work. And, best of all, Saddlebreds have a great personality that keeps them calm in noisy, crowded conditions. Saddlebreds are very friendly and approachable for kids and others on the police beat.

Rock Creek Horse Show, Louisville, Kentucky.

RECORDS AND CHAMPIONS

Prior to 1917 many great horse shows — the St. Louis Fair, American Royal, Chicago International, the Missouri and Indiana State Fairs — claimed World's Championships for various classes of Saddlebreds.

In 1916 a Missouri magazine editor and publisher, Jumps Cauthorn, having received many advertisements for "World's Champions" from different owners, decided that a means of settling on a World's Champion was long overdue. A group of Missouri horsemen agreed to this idea and attempted to raise the money for a $10,000 stake. They raised $5,000, and Cauthorn went to the Missouri governor to get the other $5,000, with the idea of holding the World's Championship at the Missouri State Fair. The Missouri governor turned the plan down, however. Enter Matt Cohen, who was at the time Kentucky's Commissioner of Agriculture and a friend of Cauthorn's. A horseman himself, Cohen liked the idea, raised the needed money, and installed the "World's Championship," as it was advertised, at the Kentucky State Fair in 1917. The first championship involved five gaited horses only; three gaited and fine harness championships were added some twenty years later.

The records that follow are limited by space to the five gaited, three gaited and fine harness open champions at the Kentucky State Fair and its predecessors, and equitation winners. Records for the amateur and pleasure divisions are available from industry sources and the American Saddlebred Horse Association.

CH Belle Elegant, ridden by Jack Nevitt

FIVE GAITED GRAND CHAMPIONS

CH Denmark's Daydream, ridden
by Lee Roby

1902	Preston 922 by Washington
1903	Rex Peavine 1796 by Rex McDonald
1904	No Fair Held
1905	Bourbon King 1788 by Bourbon Chief
1906	Indian Boy 2013 by Indian Chief, Jr.
1907	Star McDonald 1712 by Rex McDonald
1908	Red McDonald 2554 by McDonald Chief
1909	Edna May 5703 by Rex Peavine
1910	Bourbon Prince 2144 by Bourbon Chief
1911	Nickel Plate 4456 by King Lee Rose
1912	Hazel Dawn (Reg. as Rexola) 7154 by Rex Peavine
1913	Hazel Dawn
1914	Jack Barrymore 6339 by McDonald Chief
1915	Astral King 2805 by Bourbon King
1916	Richlieu King 3042 by Bourbon King
1917	Easter Cloud 4128 by McDonald Chief
1918	Cascade 6381 by King Lee Rose
1919	Liberty Girl 13836 by Rex Peavine
1920	Mass of Gold by Rex Peavine
1921	Mass of Gold
1922	Easter Star 7367 by Bourbon Star
1923	Mass of Gold
1924	Edna May's King 8672 by Bourbon King
1925	Vendetta 15081 by My McDonald
1926	Edna May's King
1927	Dark Rex 8699 by Rex Peavine
1928	Chief of Longview 9704 by Independence Chief
1929	Chief of Longview
1930	Beau Wolf by My Best Choice
1931	Sweetheart On Parade 20872 by Lee Rose McDonald
1932	Sweetheart On Parade
1933	Belle Le Rose 21495 by American Born
1934	Belle Le Rose
1935	Night Flower 20736 by Independence Chief
1936	Chief of Spindle Top 12934 by My Major Sunwise
1937	Delaine Hours (Reg. as Astral White Sox) 10516 by Astral Peavine
1938	Midnight Star by Bourbon Star
1939	Lady Jane 30657 by Independence Chief
1940	A Sensation 33597 by Oklahoma Peavine
1941	A Sensation
1942	No Fair Held Because of World War II
1943	Oak Hill Chief 26518 by Stonewall King
1944	Easter Serenade 26912 by Arletha's Easter Cloud
1945	Oak Hill Chief
1946	Oak Hill Chief
1947	Daneshall's Easter Parade 42943 by Masked Marvel
1948	Wing Commander 22591 by Anacacho Shamrock

1949   Wing Commander
1950   Wing Commander
1951   Wing Commander
1952   Wing Commander
1953   Wing Commander
1954   Lady Carrigan 46837 by Society Rex
1955   Lady Carrigan
1956   Dream Waltz 50469 by Anacacho Shamrock
1957   Lady Carrigan
1958   Lady Carrigan
1959   Plainview's Julia 53594 by Genius of Kentucky
1960   Plainview's Julia
1961   Denmark's Daydream 54595 by Anacacho Denmark
1962   Denmark's Daydream
1963   My-My 58720 by Beau Fortune
1964   My-My
1965   My-My
1966   My-My
1967   My-My
1968   My-My
1969   Valerie Emerald 90523 by Wing Commander
1970   CH Yorktown 47150 by Wing Commander
1971   CH Yorktown
1972   CH Yorktown
1973   CH Val-Dale's Surefire 63324 by Denmark's Golden Sun
1974   CH Val-Dale's Surefire
1975   CH Belle Elegant 81670 by Oman's Desdemona Denmark
1976   CH Will Shriver 50225 by Callaway's Johnny Gillen
1977   CH Belle Elegant
1978   CH Cora's Time 75825 by Flight Time
1979   CH Mountain Highland Encore 57451 by Genius Mountain Bourbon
1980   CH Imperator 64798 by Supreme Sultan
1981   CH Imperator
1982   CH Sky Watch 69166 by Flight Time
1983   CH Sky Watch
1984   CH Sky Watch
1985   CH Imperator
1986   CH Imperator
1987   CH Our Golden Duchess 94934 by Spring Valley's Deliverance
1988   CH Sky Watch
1989   CH Man On The Town 82326 by CH Yorktown
1990   CH Man On The Town
1991   CH Callaway's New Look 84893 by CH Will Shriver

CH Plainview's Julia, ridden by Lee Shipman

THREE GAITED GRAND CHAMPIONS

*CH Lover's Sensation, ridden by
Earl Teater*

1902	Gayety 1786 by Highland Denmark
1903	Gayety
1904	No Fair Held
1905	Gamblebar 1676 by Logan Denmark
1906	Poetry of Motion 3825 by King Marvel
1907	Jane S 1965 by Chester Dare
1908	Poetry of Motion
1909	Princess Sonia 5056 by Chester Dare
1910	Gladys L. 3009 by Montgomery Chief
1911	Diana Of The Lea 6049 by Rex Peavine
1912	Mildred C. 4991 by Bourbon King
1913	Kentucky's Selection 9972 by My Own Kentucky
1914	Clara Belle by Highland Gay
1915	Mary Yandell Fox 9990 by Rex Prince Dare
1916	Pretty Baby by Grand McDonald
1917	Shadow Lawn by McDonald Chief
1918	Found At Last
1919	The Answer 8516 by Raven Bird
1920	Twilight Hour 8530 by Pat Washington
1921	In Demand 8669 by Bourbon King
1922	Sporty McGee
1923	Smilin' Thru 16001 by Young Red Peavine
1924	San Marcos 7379 by Highland Squirrel King
1925	Bohemian Actress 10864 by Bohemian King
1926	Jonquil 14648 by Rex Monroe
1927	Jonquil
1928	Jonquil
1929	Jonquil
1930	Roxie Highland 15855 by Lord Highland
1931	Tee Caddy 10334 by Ben Sory
1932	Mountain Echo 11917 by Victor Peavine
1933	Roxie Highland
1934	Roxie Highland
1935	Fiery Crags
1936	American Model 10870 by American Born
1937	Morelaid Maid 25179 by American Born
1938	Golden Avalanche by Astral Peavine
1939	Golden Avalanche
1940	America Beautiful 41623 by Desert Song
1941	America Beautiful
1942	No Fair Held Because of World War II
1943	America Beautiful
1944	America Beautiful
1945	Edith Fable 28563 by American Ace
1946	Edith Fable
1947	Nellie Pidgeon 35064 by Kalarama Rex
1948	My Smoke Dreams 43905 by Kalarama Rex
1949	Magnolia's Ann Rutledge 31876 by Torpedo

1950	Blue Meadow Princess 40823 by Blue Meadow King
1951	Blue Meadow Princess
1952	Blue Meadow Princess
1953	Blue Meadow Princess
1954	Blue Meadow Princess
1955	Emerald Future 39331 by Anderson Rex
1956	Valley View Supreme 37275 by Genius Bourbon King
1957	Sunshine Carol (Reg. as Carol Carson) 48598 by Starheart Stonewall
1958	Technistar 59636 by Starheart Stonewall
1959	Delightful Society 54350 by Society Rex
1960	Delightful Society
1961	Belle of the Dell 56745 by King Coe
1962	Belle of the Dell
1963	Miss Helen 65603 by King of Rose-A-Lee
1964	Local Talent 59381 by American Dictator
1965	Local Talent
1966	Forest Song 65869 by Broadlands Captain Denmark
1967	CH Bellisima 65200 by Valley View Supreme
1968	CH Bellisima
1969	CH Bellisima
1970	CH Lover's Sensation 64375 by Vanity's Sensation of Crebilly
1971	CH Sea of Secrets 49550 by Secret Society
1972	Forest Song
1973	CH Oak Hill's Dear One 75057 by Denmark's Bourbon Genius
1974	CH Oak Hill's Dear One
1975	CH Finisterre's Gift of Love 89577 by Night of Folly
1976	CH Finisterre's Gift of Love
1977	CH Finisterre's Gift of Love
1978	CH Finisterre's Gift of Love
1979	CH Happy Valley Treasure 62229 by The Contract's Commander
1980	CH Seymour's Finest Hour 60618 by Stonewall's Main Event
1981	CH Home Town Hero 64873 by CH Yorktown
1982	CH Home Town Hero
1983	CH Sultan's Starina 94647 by Supreme Sultan
1984	Ch Sultan's Starina
1985	CH Sultan's Starina
1986	CH Sultan's Starina
1987	CH Sultan's Starina
1988	Black Irish 69078 by Stonewall's Crescendo
1989	CH Gimcrack 79439 by Jamestown
1990	CH Cameo's Angel Wings 104059 by Wing Shot
1991	CH One For The Road 87617 by Supreme Heir

CH Delightful Society, ridden by Eddie Boyd

FINE HARNESS GRAND CHAMPIONS

*CH Colonel Boyle, Arthur
Simmons Driving*

1902   Miss Peabody 1978 by Big Jim
1903   Kentucky's Belle 1598 by Red Eagle
1904   No Fair Held
1905   The American Girl 3024 by Montgomery Chief
1906   Nominee 1596 by Chester Dare
1907   Top 2438 by Cleveland Dare
1908   Kate Hamilton 6416 by Bracken Chief
1909   Golden Glow 3962 by Rex Peavine
1910   Nazimova 5041 by Montgomery Chief
1911   Nazimova
1912   Jaqueline 9683 by Rex Peavine
1913   Kentucky's Best 5664 by My Own Kentucky
1914   Sun Flower 4660 by Highland Flower
1915   Dixie Highway
1916   Lady Beautiful 12865 by Rex Peavine
1917   Lady Beautiful
1918   Maydan 7400 by Jack Twigg
1919   Lady Beautiful
1920   Lady Beautiful
1921   Lady Beautiful
1922   Elizabeth Greis (Reg. as Phoebe Dare) 14167 by
        Limestone McDonald
1923   Violet Heming 15273 by McDonald McDonald
1924   Emily McCready 14323 by Bourbon King
1925   Peavine's Dream 9103 by Wizzim
1926   La Grita
1927   Suttie Leigh 15266 by Sun Flower
1928   Lulworth Victor 9011 by Bugger Boo
1929   Charming Gypsy 16630 by King Barrymore
1930   Supreme (Reg. as California Star) 10501 by Edna
        May's King
1931   Chief of Longview
1932   Chief of Longview
1933   Fiery Crags 13267 by Mountain Star
1934   Allen Adair 11024 by Kalarama Rex
1935   Allen Adair
1936   Allen Adair
1937   Bourbon Genius 13411 by King's Genius
1938   Meadow Vanity 23974 by Meadow Majesty
1939   Meadow Vanity
1940   Noble Kalarama 12395 by Kalarama Rex
1941   Meadow Vanity
1942   No Fair Held Because of World War II
1943   Meadow Vanity
1944   Meadow Vanity
1945   Captain Bird 19225 by Captain Courageous
1946   Startling Kalarama 19272 by Kalarama Rex
1947   Regal Aire (Reg. as Denmark's Mokanna) 21745 by
        Anacacho Denmark

1948   Man of the Hour (Reg. as Captain Dandy) 20936 by Cracker Barrymore
1949   Kate Shriver 43606 by Anacacho Denmark
1950   Kate Shriver
1951   Parading Lady by Denmark Beaverkettle
1952   Parading Lady
1953   Regal Aire
1954   Parading Lady
1955   High Button Shoes (Reg. as Bit O'Chatter) 32392 by Cameo Kirby
1956   The Lemon Drop Kid 33797 by Cameo Kirby
1957   The Lemon Drop Kid
1958   The Lemon Drop Kid
1959   The Lemon Drop Kid
1960   Colonel Boyle 37752 by Kalarama Colonel
1961   Colonel Boyle
1962   Colonel Boyle
1963   Colonel Boyle
1964   Colonel Boyle
1965   The Thunderbird 41455 by Starheart Stonewall
1966   CH Duke of Daylight 42195 by Majestic Ensign
1967   CH Duke of Daylight
1968   CH Tashi Ling 61338 by Wing Commander
1969   CH Tashi Ling
1970   CH Tashi Ling
1971   CH Tashi Ling
1972   CH Supreme Airs 62778 by Stonewall Supreme
1973   CH Glenview Mandala 79454 by Stonewall's Beau Peavine
1974   CH Reata's Virginia Wolf 72910 by Oman's Desdemona Denmark
1975   CH Ronald Reagan 51589 by Stonewall's Beau Peavine
1976   CH Night Prowler 59129 by Status Symbol
1977   CH Melody's Winged Sensation 52931 by Vanity's Sensation of Crebilly
1978   CH Melody's Winged Sensation
1979   CH La La Success 84449 by Stonewall's Main Event
1980   CH La La Success
1981   Sultan's Santana 58735 by Supreme Sultan
1982   CH Shadow's Creation 67589 by Supreme's Shadow
1983   CH Night Prowler
1984   CH Vanity's Showcase 97497 by Folly's Night Flyer
1985   CH Vanity's Showcase
1986   CH Vanity's Showcase
1987   CH Captive Spirit 78227 by CH Kourageous Kalu
1988   CH Buck Rogers 73982 by Storm's Fury
1989   CH Foxfire's Prophet 82409 by Radiant Sultan
1990   CH Simply Mahvalous B.R. 86042 by Sultan's Great Day
1991   CH Roselawn's Secret Rhythm 81156 by Tijuana Rhythm

CH Vanity's Showcase, Larry Hodge driving

EQUITATION CHAMPIONS

NATIONAL HORSE SHOW EQUITATION CHAMPIONSHIP SADDLE SEAT (GOOD-HANDS)

1990 Allison Beard	1977 Carol Reams	1964 Randi Stuart	1951 Skipper Schroeder	1938 Arthur Plaut
1989 Ann Luise Montgomery	1976 Virginia Cable	1963 Sue Ellen Marshall	1950 Gail Fenbert	1937 Marci Murray
1988 Catherine Schuessler	1975 Ann Swisher	1962 Nancy Ripa	1949 Janet Sage *	1936 Margaret Augusta Seavers
1987 Kate Harvey	1974 Linda Lowary	1961 Sarah Nutting	1948 Barbara Pease	1935 Rosamond F. Murray **
1986 Susan Cole	1973 Dana Lyon	1960 Vicki Reiter	1947 Elaine Shirley Watt	1934 Walter Perry Davis
1985 Kelly Gilligan	1972 Mary Lib DeNure	1959 Jan Casler	1946 Albert Torek	1933 Rosamond F. Murray **
1984 Megan Stuart	1971 Judy Maccari	1958 Linda Frankel	1945 Dorothy Van Winkle	1932 Louise Finch
1983 Jana Weir	1970 Susie Maccari	1957 Stephanie Robin Kob	1944 Nancy Dean ***	1931 Rosamond F. Murray **
1982 Jama Hedden	1969 Janet Henry	1956 Luann Beach	1943 Anne Ritterbush	1930 Edith Gould Anderson
1981 Kathy Jo Thompson	1968 Jennifer Miller	1955 Mikee McCormack	1942 George McKelvey	* Only rider to win riding
1980 Janice Christensen	1967 Andrea Walton	1954 Martin Rosenweig	1941 William C. Steinkraus ***	sidesaddle
1979 Shanna Schoonmaker	1966 Judy Fisher	1953 Janice Weitz	1940 James A. Thomas, Jr. ***	** Rider could win more than one
1978 Mary Lou Gallagher	1965 Edward Lumia	1952 Diana Brown	1939 Muriel Arthur	year
				*** Riders won "Good Hands" &
				ASPCA Maclay trophies

AHSA SADDLE SEAT MEDAL FINALS CHAMPIONS

1990 Allison Beard	1981 Neil Anne Perrey	1972 Judy Maccari	1963 Randi Stuart	1954 Martin Rosenweig
1989 Erin Swope	1980 Janice Christensen	1971 Susie Maccari	1962 Cathlyn Patrick	1953 Roberta Smith
1988 Catherine Schuessler	1979 Ashley Tway	1970 Julee Lampkin	1961 Gloria Green	1952 Barbara Clevely
1987 Kate Harvey	1978 Dabney Cubbage	1969 Barbara Hoffman	1960 Mary Anne O'Callaghan	1951 Gail Fenbert
1986 Nancy Orscheln	1977 Carol Reams	1968 Janet Henry	1959 Brienne Jorgensen	1950 Carol Kruse
1985 Kelly Gilligan	1976 Virginia Cable	1967 Judy Fisher	1958 Lynne Girdler	1949 Alice Gudebrad
1984 Cameron Martin	1975 Kate Williams	1966 Andrea Walton	1957 Kathy Whiteside	1948 Corinne Hoffman
1983 Megan Stuart	1974 Mary Lib DeNure	1965 Edward Lumia	1956 Luann Beach	* 1948 - marked 1st year for 3
1982 Jama Hedden	1973 Dana Lyon	1964 Julianne Schmutz	1955 Sandra Harris	separate divisions (stock, saddle &
				hunt seats).

UPHA NATIONAL CHALLENGE CUP CHAMPIONS

1990 Nicole Jackson	1986 Betsey Kiltz-Stallings	1982 Jama Hedden	1978 Todd Buchanan	1974 Mary Lib DeNure
1989 Anne Luis Montgomery	1985 Nancy Orscheln	1981 Kathy Jo Thompson	1977 Shauna Schoonmaker	1973 Sherrie Phelps
1988 Catherine Schuessler	1984 Kelly Gilligan	1980 Janice Christensen	1976 Ann Swisher	1972 Judy Maccari
1987 Kate Harvey	1983 Christie Fletcher	1979 Diane Caldemeyer	1975 Elizabeth Finch	

UPHA JUNIOR CHALLENGE CUP CHAMPIONS

1990 Taja Bleu Setzer	1987 Lindsay Lavery	1985 Anne Luis Montgomery	1983 Cameron Martin	1981 Ruth Anne Lewis
1989 Elizabeth Ghareeb	1986 Catherine Schuesselr	1984 Courtney Malowney	1982 Kate Harvey	1980 Jama Hedden
1988 Mary Jane Glasscock				1979 Kendy Almeida

UPHA 10 & UNDER WALK/TROT CHALLENGE CUP CHAMPIONS

1990 Bryant Belte	1989 Cindy Sherman	1988 Toni Knight

PLEASURE EQUITATION NATIONAL CHAMPIONS

1990 Nichole Bearman	1987 Nicole Jackson	1984 Julie Morgan	1981 Peg Paulas	1979 Sandy Bernd
1989 Donna Pettry	1986 Nicole Jackson	1983 Robin Frakes	1980 Lisa Petro	1978 Denise Lullo
1988 Neva LaFleur	1985 Debbie Dickerson	1982 Jill Baahlman		

PLEASURE EQUITATION OLYMPICS

1990 Mechelle Pocock *	1989 Beth Ann Gulick *	1988 Alexa Loudon *	1987 Melissa Pappas *	* 13 & Under
Nicole Bearman**	Donna Pettry **	Robin Schultz **	Nicole Jackson **	** 14 - 17

SADDLE & BRIDLE PLEASURE EQUITATION MEDALLION FINALS

1990 Julie Ann Marrett	1987 Liv LaFleur	1985 Debbie Dickerson	1983 Jackie Erdman	1981 Tiffany Dickerson
1989 Courtenay Lancaster	1986 Blake Cornell	1984 Robert Griffin	1982 Janet Crampton	1980 Peg Paulas
1988 Michele Powell				1979 Sandy Bernd

NATIONAL PLEASURE EQUITATION OLYMPICS

1990 Mechelle Pocock *	1989 Beth Ann Gulick *	1988 Alexa Louden *	1987 Melissa Pappas *	* 13 & Under
Nicole Bearman **	Donna Pettry **	Robin Shultz **	Nicole Jackson **	** 14 - 17